Advance Praise

I have been fortunate to work with MaryBeth and the SparkVision team twice—in two nonprofit, mission-based organizations—to define and adopt organizational values and to operationalize healthy and sustainable culture shifts. In only a year, our team has embraced the values we forged together as foundational to our internal culture and as inspirational to our work. The beauty of her book is that it combines the wisdom of her intuitive gifts with proven practices about how diverse groups of individuals can take the journey together, particularly in times of stress, and embrace what once seemed impossible. As an executive leader, I wish this book had been available decades ago!

—Lisa M. Schroeder, president and CEO, The Pittsburgh Foundation

Technology is transforming every single job on the planet and will replace millions of them in the upcoming years. However, we have an unbeatable competitive advantage over technology: it can't do what humans are unique and extraordinary at—that is, being human. *Permission to Be Human* is a timely and necessary guide for leaders to heighten their EQ, systems, and processes for our shared human experience at work.

—Enrique Rubio, founder, Hacking HR

MaryBeth is a powerful, empathic, and conscious leader who both lives by her core values and is here to activate more consciousness in the workplace. In *Permission to Be Human*, she makes the case for activating our hearts more intentionally so that we can all thrive at work today and for generations to come. MaryBeth walks the walk of living in alignment with the highest values for thriving teams, companies, and humanity.

—Julie Reisler, international transformation coach

PERMISSION TO BE HUMAN

Permission to Be Human

The Conscious Leader's Guide to Creating a Values-Driven Culture

By MaryBeth Hyland

SparkVision Publishing

Hardback - ISBN: 978-1-7372888-0-0
Paperback - ISBN: 978-1-7372888-1-7
e-book/Digital Online - ISBN: 978-1-7372888-2-4

To my husband, James, for being my greatest champion in life, for knowing my work had the power to change lives before I did, and for always sitting with and supporting me when I doubt it. Thank you for being the mirror in showing me just how good life can be when you know, own, and live your values.

Table of Contents

Foreword

The exercise was simple enough. A nonprofit led a group of leaders through a poverty simulation to ignite insight into and to dialogue about how to support people facing the complex reality of this daily struggle.

I already knew what it took to succeed in an environment of poverty. Although today I am a senior vice president at Booz Allen Hamilton and former executive at Lockheed Martin, my values were forged from my humble beginnings in East Baltimore. Baltimore, like most urban cities, is made up of people who go to work every day, raise their families, and love deeply. They learn to thrive despite the many socioeconomic, political, and educational hardships they endure. During the exercise, I was reminded of what it was like to have parents work multiple jobs, support their children's education, and suffer the frustrations of networking through systems that are supposed to support them but that often do not.

As I watched my fellow executive participants role-play, I noticed that it didn't take long for them to feel overwhelmed. Their level of education didn't matter. Their forceful and authoritative voices could neither bring a social services employee back early from their lunch break nor force public transportation to move at the speed needed to get back to work on time so that they wouldn't lose their job. They saw that teachers were making decisions that were not in their children's best interests and realized the heartache of not being able to take time off from their second job in order to attend a parent-teacher conference in order to voice and resolve the issues.

It was powerful, memorable, and uniting.

It was during this exercise when I first noticed MaryBeth's passion for people, her passion for relationships, her passion for what makes us human. She was leading the session and helped us all to see that in the face of adversity, our values are the common thread that link us to our humanity and to each other.

Soon after, she started her own business that facilitated immersive work in order to ignite new connections. But now it wasn't a simulation of other people's lives; it was a deep dive into the mirror to see ourselves more fully and to bring people closer by sharing the stories of our truth. These actions are at the heart of giving ourselves permission to be who we really are. That level of authenticity is the very heart of being human.

It is the struggle to be human that brings us all together. As you'll learn in this book, MaryBeth is on a mission to guide others on a mindful journey to be more authentic, whole, and empowered humans—especially at work.

Like me, she knew that too many superficial interactions led to disengagement, dissatisfaction, and disconnection. The world needs people to have the skills, tools, and language to develop deeper relationships. MaryBeth makes that possible through her guidance in assisting us in knowing, owning, and living our core values.

Throughout my career, I have had the privilege of working with some of the smartest people in the world to create technology that addresses the most critical issues. Together, we have leveraged the intersection of technology, strategy, and business to create and capture value, lead innovation, and drive execution.

As a leader today, I know that my values are a reflection of those that I saw growing up in Baltimore. My values are rooted in the deep conviction of hard work, respect, and helping others. MaryBeth taught me how to consciously align actions with values. She has also helped my team to be courageous enough to be vulnerable and empathetic by sharing themselves through the stories of our collective shared values.

When I spearheaded a new cyber innovations team, my desire was for the newly formed team to be dynamic collaborators. In order for us to thrive, we had to connect deeply and quickly. I knew that it was the ideal time to strategically partner with MaryBeth. She could make that happen.

Right from the start, she immediately connected and committed herself to the group. Her deep expert knowledge of the subject matter was evident as she led multiple staff retreats and facilitated conversations and workshops. But it was her compassion for each individual and our collective mission that made her an honorary member of our team. She brought a new thinking about our challenges and led us to develop a values manifesto that laid the foundation of how we would interact with each other and our broader teams. During a closeout session, one of my tenured executives shared that MaryBeth's work with us was some of the deepest and most innovative ways of connecting that they ever experienced in their career.

I know what highly motivated and connected teams can do. And I know how demotivated and disconnected teams can suffer. I have learned that good leadership is about building and motivating a team around a common vision and mission. I have also learned that activating our shared values and being our true selves is at the heart of team building, loyalty, and engagement. People give their best when their values are activated and when they feel valued in return. By giving ourselves permission to be human, we create environments where people have a sense of passion, purpose, and alignment. This is massively important when it comes to our leadership and culture at work.

As you'll soon learn in the pages to come, MaryBeth is an authority and thought leader in this space. I have experienced the extremely positive results of the tenets of this book. *Permission to Be Human* will soon become required reading for leaders looking to build people, teams, and relationships.

—*Dr. Charles Johnson-Bey, senior vice president, Booz Allen Hamilton*

Introduction

This book is a love letter to any fellow humans who have felt like they were the underdogs for deeply caring about people and their well-being at work.

I used to be so shocked by how few people knew how to treat others. I spent years feeling like a loner; I even began to think I had a chemical imbalance or something. Up until I went to therapy, I lived a psychologically heavy life thinking that something was wrong with me because of the lack of emotional reciprocation from others that just felt "normal" to me.

And now I know, with incredible confidence, that's 100 percent BS.

We're all taught the golden rule: "Treat people the way you want to be treated." But how can you treat others the way you want to be treated when in reality you have no idea how you really want to be treated? You just know you don't want to feel pain but are unsure of what the other end of that spectrum looks, feels, and sounds like because you haven't experienced it before.

If we're never taught to tap into who we are authentically, then we're simply making educated guesses on our life choices based on other people's opinions of who *they* want us to be and what would make *them* feel proud of us. So many of us are living out the lives, careers, and titles that other people wanted for us, but we have never really tapped in to see if that's what we want for ourselves—let alone figured out what makes us feel a sense of purpose, alignment, and aliveness.

And what is almost never shared in a "professional setting" is that those very gifts are often born of our greatest burdens.

My dad was a product of childhood abuse. Sadly, it became the parenting style he chose to carry on as my father. Out of fear of being hurt, he taught me how to morph myself into someone he approved of. And when that didn't happen, his wounds rose to the surface with intensity. The pain that lived inside him was one that I typically knew how to soothe with laughter, with responsibility, with precision and love. I know that my behavior was mostly a matter of survival. And looking back now, I can see how brave that scared little girl was. She stood next to the roaring monster, and instead of running away to hide, she stayed still while he snarled, and she said in her actions and behaviors, "It's OK. We're OK. What can I do to help you realize that you don't have to be scary? What can I do to help you know that you're loved? How can I shift the energy between us so that we can both be at peace?"

And by some miracle, eight out of ten times, that little girl was a success.

That same emotionally intelligent little girl was labeled a crybaby, incredibly sensitive, overly emotional, and too caring. These classifications of weakness followed me throughout my adulthood and career.

Now I know that those were shame tools that made me see my gifts as burdens. They made me believe that these qualities were something that was *wrong* with me instead of what was so very *right* inside of me.

Perhaps you can relate with your own unique version of this story. Have you ever felt like you were the oddball for being the one who cared about people "too much"?

Well, I'm here to shout from the rooftops with you: *"You're a gift! Your sensitivities are a superpower! The world needs your feelings and your voice to share them! Keep going; I promise, it gets better!"* I know how exhausting it can be to feel like the only one who "gets it," especially at work—but there's hope!

When I was a young professional, my career path consisted of one- to two-year jobs that I either loved but were temporary or in which I was miserable and left because the culture was so toxic that it made me physically and mentally ill. Over time it became apparent that my supervisors' emotional intelligence and personal well-being played a large role in whether I'd be able to last.

Before starting my business in 2015, I was working at a local nonprofit that had a global presence. At the time, it was the largest nonprofit in the world, and I was proud to be one of their kick-ass fundraisers.

While managing campaigns, I watched their young-professional program limp its way through each month. And I yearned for the opportunity to give it the structure and engagement that I knew it deserved. I had a strong internal pull. I knew it would take only some small, intentional tweaks to make a big impact—igniting a millennial movement the global organization had never witnessed before.

My obvious desire to spark my vision was met with the opportunity to inherit the program. I was given the chance to do what I thought was best, within reason, to shift the program. Membership quadrupled in one year, and six months later, the headquarters deemed it a global best practice model for young-professional engagement.

I was equal parts thrilled and confused—well, maybe it skewed more toward the *thrilled* side. How had I, in such a short time frame, been able to influence other chapters that had been doing the work much longer?

That question was answered in the months to follow. You see, once you are flagged as a best practice model, every time a local chapter calls headquarters asking for help with young professionals, they refer them to you directly. I was getting calls from all over the world wanting to get ahold of my secret sauce for millennial engagement!

After coaching, leading workshops, and giving speeches, I had an epiphany. There was a massive deficit of knowledge on how to intentionally craft a culture that attracted and retained young professionals. Most people felt perplexed by what my generation craved in engagement and could not figure out step one in that process.

From years of having the same conversations, I realized how prevalent the disconnect was with understanding how to intentionally craft a culture in which people felt good. It was such a strong realization that it gave me the knowledge and firsthand expertise I needed to launch my consulting firm, SparkVision, which works with individuals and organizations all over the world to create environments where people can thrive. I was divinely positioned to help more people understand how they are a vital piece of crafting the cultures around them every day.

I had a great reputation and network, so leaving the nonprofit was a beautiful transition that nonetheless had its challenges.

At first all the new inquiries I received sounded something like this: "These millennials in my office are so entitled and think they're going to be the CEO within weeks of being employed. Can you come and fix that?" Or "Kids these days have no respect for the way things are done around here. I don't know what to do."

And finally, "I got a Ping-Pong table, started jeans Fridays, and created unlimited vacation. Why aren't millennials happy here?"

If anyone made comments like these, I would listen intently and openly (the latter was trying at times) because it was these questions and statements that ultimately got my foot in the door to talk about what I really stood for—the core of the disconnect.

When I'd come in for a formal meeting, I'd wind up telling them that I did not recommend happy hours, free lunches, and beanbag chairs but instead recommended focusing on the things that they stood for. What was—unshakably—who they were? What mattered to them without exception? In other words, what were their core values, and how could we create a culture that reflected these values?

Through these efforts, what I now know for sure is that it is not a millennial thing. It's a human thing.

Generally speaking, we humans all want the same things. We each have a different tolerance level regarding how long we're able to put up with what we don't want. And although we might not be able to articulate it, we all want to work in a culture that is driven by shared values and accountability, that creates a sense of belonging and purpose. Using those very basic human concepts, I won a state- and sector-wide Innovator of the Year Award.

It is now my life's work to create the space for moving from frustration to understanding, from surviving to thriving—with each of us owning our roles in creating the culture that surrounds us. When we get curious about our perspectives, values, and gifts, we can learn that it's not as complicated as it feels in our heads. That's why I'm so passionate about this work. It takes the complex and makes it simple.

It's not so much that I'm a hard-core values advocate as I am passionate about the opening that they create. Values are not just values, but rather they are the key to unlocking the emotional intelligence that already exists within us. When using values as their guide, people are able to tap into parts of themselves that may have been dormant for years by simply asking them to reflect on what matters most to them.

This book will teach you how to double down on harnessing your emotional intelligence in order to understand your own humanity and therefore the humanity of your team and company at large. Whether you're a founder of an organization or the leader of a team, you will be the head culture keeper of your environment from a place of confidence and grace.

Just imagine with me now...

What if people finally woke up to understanding that their behaviors affect everyone around them? And what if they had the tools to learn how to evolve?

What if people understood that they are simply and completely walking, talking, living, breathing sets of values? And what if they knew that their companies were too?

What if even 10 percent of companies *lived, breathed,* and *activated* their shared core values every single day at work? And what would be the ripple effects of this change in communities outside of work?

It sends chills up my spine thinking that you and I now have the honor of making an impact by helping people to wake up and stop being victims by giving them the tools to take action on what they want to change in their workplaces. I want you to feel supported in your journey and open to doing the work that's required to create environments that are rooted in love, not fear.

This book will give you a chance to see yourself and your teammates through a new lens: the lens of our shared human experience and the values that live within every action and behavior—ingrained or aspirational—of your workplace culture. Ultimately, I'll guide you through becoming fluent in the language of values so that you can articulate them from a place of intention, tune in to your intuition, and confront your shadow—the unconscious sides of yourself—to create alignment between your values and your behaviors.

David Swirnow, the CEO of Swirnow Building Systems, one of my long-term clients in the construction industry, said of our partnership in a meeting, "Your work has given us permission to be human, and I didn't know that was possible here." It was so significant that team members repeated the phrase back so that we could all let it sink in. We knew it was the whole point of doing the work and feeling proud of its influence. His vulnerable and genuine share inspired the title of this book. As you read, you will learn how to give yourself and others permission to be human too!

The concept of permission to be human has several meanings to me. I hope these interpretations will give you some insight into the lens through which I wrote this book. For starters, "permission" is profound for us humans. We often hold ourselves back for lack of permission or for believing that it's not OK for us to be a certain way. In order to unconditionally give anyone else permission, we have to first give that permission to ourselves. In the mindfulness community, "to be" is to exist. It's a reminder that we're human beings, not human doings, and that our greatest well-being emerges when we choose to become conscious through inner stillness. And then finally, "human" is the great bond between us. We have loads of differences but significantly more similarities in our human experience. When we share our life experiences, we inevitably find that we're all connected.

I've even created the following Permission to Be Human Pledge, which I encourage people to recite as much as possible. Try reading this next section with your hand on your heart, and see how it impacts you:

I promise to honor what makes me perfectly imperfect.

I promise to meet myself where I am, not where I want to be.

I promise to suspend judgment and ignite compassion.

I promise to set healthy boundaries to protect my energy.

I promise to prioritize my well-being by embodying my values.

And in doing so, I promise to give myself and others permission to be human.

Throughout this text, you'll find the header "Give permission to be human" or simply "Permission to be human." In those areas, I'm focusing the lens on the thought process I just outlined. My intention is to keep reminding you that to sustainably change anything for the better, we must give ourselves and others full permission to be human. The nuances are vast, which is why those sections are important to note and remind yourself of as you go on your journey. To give permission to be human is to have radical compassion to exist as you are, not who or where you want to be.

As a millennial engagement specialist who has since evolved into a human engagement expert, I know that values-driven cultures are the cultures that most business leaders are deeply interested in. The shame is that very few take action on that interest. Many are willing to hire a branding consultant to pick the words that wind up on their office walls with fancy posters, but in that process, they often lose the heart of the workplace. It's a box-checking exercise, a one-and-done experience. And that's just not how values work. They live within us forever, every single day. The companies that are activating those (potentially dormant) ties to our sense of purpose are unleashing incredible new possibilities. When you genuinely invest in the time and resources to learn what intrinsically motivates your people, you can uncover the values that unify everyone. Intrinsic motivators are behaviors that are driven by internal rewards. There's no comparison to the positive feelings you experience when your values are honored.

Values-driven cultures matter today more than ever. Artificial intelligence is on the rise, and lived *human* values will be increasingly important as functional tasks are commandeered by nonhuman actors. Social media and technology are exponentially taking over our attention, making the physical and cognitive disconnect a greater barrier to break down. It is urgent that we reignite the one-to-one human connection based on our shared values. At the time of this book's release, we are still evolving our way through the coronavirus pandemic. The clearly visible prospect of work staying remote and workplaces becoming more dispersed underlines the need for values as a bonding agent. *Now is our time to come together in our shared humanity by knowing, owning, and living our values at work.*

I will guide you in this process, but you have to be committed to the journey, to be willing to fall down and get up and do that forever. That's how culture goes—it exists every day, whether you do something about it or not. Together, we'll choose better, for you, for your people, and for your company—over and over again.

Section I:
Know Your Values

CHAPTER 1

The Evolution of Workplace Culture

No problem can be solved at the same level of consciousness that created it.
—Albert Einstein

When I was growing up, this is how I believed that work went:

Step 1: Discover your gifts.

Step 2: Get hired for your passion and skills.

Step 3: Stay at the same workplace decade after decade, making a lasting difference in other people's lives, and get paid to do what you love alongside your "work family."

Superrealistic, right? That was all my mom's fault!

My mom was a superhero—not by trade, but I saw her that way because she helped people who had come undone feel whole again. As a leading art therapist, she worked with people who had mental illness who often felt unheard, unimportant, and even forgotten, helping to heal them using clay, pastels, watercolor, collages, and dialogue. Like I said, Mom was a superhero.

When I was twelve years old, she worked with women experiencing homelessness in Baltimore to create a huge mural of a city home with a storybook wild, yet tamed, garden full of flowers. They called it *My Sister's Garden.*

Each woman painted a flower that represented what was beautiful about her. And although together and separately they were all beautiful, most of these women had never been accepted into a curated, tamed, or tended-to home garden. They couldn't quite cross that barrier and instead lived as wildflowers, as best they could; the mural honored their struggle. It was profound for these women to be represented for their personal views and not what others assumed about them.

No wonder I thought about work as a place that valued your passion and skills. And then I got to be the superhero's sidekick.

A few days before the official mural debut and gallery exhibit, my mom enlisted my sister and me to head to our local mall and get each woman a *new* professional-looking outfit to wear at the grand opening of the mural. As I watched each woman stand next to the flower she'd painted, explaining its meaning while wearing an outfit I'd helped to pick out, I, too, felt like a superhero.

We helped these women to feel power, beauty, gratitude, and, most of all, love. It was a collaborative expression of something rich for each and every person involved. Creating those feelings and experiences was my mom's job!

My mom taught me that work isn't just work. It's passion. Of course, your job is also there to pay your bills, but she showed me that if you spend forty or more hours a week somewhere, it better be feeding your soul as much as your belly. The magical gallery-opening moments pulled you through the disappointed, loss-of-sleep moments that come with any job. But the highs were greater than the lows and ignited a sense of purpose, alignment, passion, and energy.

When I went out into the workforce, that is what I expected from my career...

Guess what? It was not quite that way. But I understood something important that I might not have if I had not witnessed my mother's work: When we go into work, we feel something energetically. Energy introduces itself before anyone even opens their mouths. It's presented through a gut feeling, an instinct, a vibe. It's why some places feel warm and inviting and others feel stale and uncomfortable. There's a pretty big energy scale, especially once people do start opening their mouths. It ranges from feeling like we are coming alive to feeling like we are being sucked dry. Those energy infusers and vampires are easy to identify when we listen to our bodies, minds, hearts, and spirits—because we pretty much always know it; we just don't always want to accept it or do the work to change it.

When you look at what creates that range of energy, it always comes down to whether your values are being activated. In other words, if you feel like you're coming alive, it's because your values are in action. And if you feel like you're being sucked dry, it's because you're being drained from a lack of your values being activated.

If that energy talk doesn't register, then how about this: You either like being there or you don't. It's that simple.

When your values are fully activated, it means that they are more than just platitudes; they are in motion, easily infused into an experience, part of the operations, and hitting on all cylinders. Say you thrive on creativity. A fully activated and aligned culture of creativity would equate to a culture in which people are empowered to make mistakes, be vulnerable, and try new things. New ideas and fresh perspectives would be expected (and not balked at), and the day-to-day flow would enable people to have the space (physically, mentally, emotionally, spiritually) to be creative. There would be budgets, hiring processes, and meeting structures that all enhance and support the ability to be creative. And when you ask other people to describe your company or product, external folks would reflect on how creative it is.

So if creativity is what gives you a feeling of aliveness, wouldn't an activated and aligned culture that knows, owns, and lives that value make you feel pretty darn awesome?

Reality Check

When I completed my bachelor's in social work and a master's in nonprofit management, I had it all planned out. At twenty-two I'd get my passion and purpose on and snag that decades-long career with cherished colleagues!

And then I entered the workforce—during the Great Recession.

I searched for jobs that resonated with me and were designed to make an impact on others' lives. To my delight, many of the job descriptions and interviews hit home. I was excited to see where I would make my mark and cultivate my work family along the way.

In the case of job after job, I came in with so much energy and optimism and then, a few months later, I felt like I had lost a bit of my soul. What was promised to me on paper and in interviews seemed like what I was born to do. Then, once I was integrated into the team, it was like I had been gaslighted.

What happened to those leaders who said they valued the opinions and skills of their employees? Where did the environment that was driven by personal and professional growth go?

How could I believe that they were telling the truth when they said I would be rewarded for my creativity?

Maybe I was just naive, too sensitive, or perhaps even entitled? In my heart I thought there was something very wrong with me because I did not love my job…in fact, my work hurt my well-being.

What I didn't know then, but what I know wholeheartedly now, is that the reason none of those jobs worked out for me was the disconnect between my core values and the values that were being practiced in the company culture.

As humans, we are all walking, talking, living, breathing sets of values. The same is true for your company. Values serve as a handshake between you and your employees on what you should expect from each other. They represent the core of the company and how you define success and failure. But all too often, they are just nice ideas.

Before I was hired, I read the job descriptions, and they checked all my boxes:

- ☑ Community facing?

- ☑ Grounded in collaboration?

- ☑ Empowered to be innovative and creative?

- ☑ Health insurance and enough pay to cover my student loans?

But then I would accept the position and learn that those job descriptions and interview promises were just facades that masked the actual company culture. All those boxes they had checked were more related to marketing collateral than to the reality of my experience.

One company claimed that it valued innovation. I presented an idea to improve an engagement system that was no longer working; I was told to stay in my lane and stop trying to make other people look bad.

Another company claimed to have the value of accountability, but I quickly learned that was only for the worker bees and not for the powers that be. Though the company had a no-cell-phones-in-meetings policy, the executives always seemed to have "an emergency" to attend to by responding to emails throughout every meeting. But if I were to pull out my phone, it would be brought up in a one-on-one as disrespectful.

And the biggest killer was with a team that claimed to swear by collaboration. I was stoked to be a part of a group that believed in dynamic conversation to ultimately land on a solution together. Welp…I quickly learned that the *same* chosen people were always pulled into those collaboration sessions, and the rest of us were left out on an island not knowing what would be dictated to us next. It was the ultimate feeling of not belonging and of being forced into a silo.

At these jobs, the environments became so toxic that I would get sick on Sunday night just thinking about five straight days of it. Their values didn't add up, and they didn't match mine. There were even occasions when I'd hide in the bathroom at work and cry, praying that no one would notice and I could get myself together quickly.

All these stories boil down to one thing: culture.

The Energy of Culture

Encyclopedia.com defines corporate culture as "the shared values, attitudes, standards, and beliefs that characterize members of an organization and define its nature. Derived from an organization's goals, strategies, structure, and approaches to labor, customers, investors, and the greater community."[1]

Add to that definition some familiar phrases about culture: "the way things are done around here," "the average of everyone," "your company's personality," "the emotional experience."

Workplace culture is all about feelings and emotions. Feelings are associated with physical body reactions—like being tired. This is why physicians ask, "How are you feeling?" Emotions are the mental associations with and reactions to feeling—like being tired because you're so drained from not being sure if you're going to get the promotion you need to afford your new car payments. This is why therapists ask, "How does that make you feel?"

More simply, feelings are the language of the body, and emotions are the translation of those feelings in the mind. Feelings cause emotions. If you're feeling filled up with energy, you'll likely activate emotions associated with productivity, accomplishment, or even passion.

What matters is the sum of the feelings and emotions you have when you're on the job and the feelings and emotions you have when thinking about work before or after you're officially on the clock. We all know that energy lingers and crosses over the superficial work-life balance lines. And they impact everyone we have contact with.

Have you been a part of a culture where you felt sick just thinking about going into work?

And what about being a part of a culture where you had butterflies in your stomach because you were so excited about what it was you were about to do?

---

1 Encyclopedia.com, "Corporate Culture," updated May 17, 2018, https://www.encyclopedia.com/social-sciences-and-law/ economics-business-and-labor/businesses-and-occupations/corporate-culture.

You know the difference between the two? Your body knows the difference; it sends you messages about whether that culture is a good fit for you.

The messages can be received through paying attention to your silent but powerful energy. Are you being filled or drained? Is your inner battery being charged or sucked dry and in need of jumper cables just to make it through the week? Ultimately, that energy tells you whether you love it, like it, or hate it there.

I used to think that culture was just something that happened. And it does, but if you are looking to revive or launch an intentional workplace experience, crafting your culture will be a practice in intention, dedication, and joy. Yeah, you read that right! When you are intentional about the space you desire to create and are dedicated to tending to that environment regularly, joy is the natural result. And joy can live only in the presence of your values.

You Can't Outsource Culture

Culture exists whether you do something about it or not. An external consultant cannot come in and "fix" it for you. You can't outsource your culture. It's impossible, since the culture is created by you and everyone else who works with you. And just like it can't be outsourced, it also can't be stolen. It's one commodity that cannot be replicated exactly or copied in a way that would take away from your own version. When a leader—like you—chooses to do something about their culture, it can shift from something that just happens to something that's purposefully created, nurtured, and sustained.

I'm often asked, "How do you get so many people involved in your programs?" And my response is always this: "I've created an intentional culture that's grounded in our values and attracts people who share them with us." Authenticity, transparency, empathy, vulnerability, accountability, and inner harmony are the foundation that we've built to create a psychologically safe space. We ask people what they want, empower them to own that solution, and then support the process for success in reaching it from a place of personal alignment.

Sounds simple, right? If it were, you likely would not be reading this book.

This seemingly simple work is complex, layered, and difficult for most people—especially for leaders like you, who want to "get it right" but need support on where to start and want guidance on understanding whether you are on the right path.

I have been the leader of a company intentionally and unintentionally crafting culture firsthand every day. And I have been a team member in a company, feeling the positive and the negative impacts of other leaders' abilities or inabilities to craft culture. Both of these important perspectives are what ultimately led me to focus my work on helping other leaders know, own, and live their values every day so that they can create thriving environments for themselves and their people.

Whether you just started your business or are about to expand, you know how vital your culture is for its sustainability. And although that is apparent, the truth is that culture has its own language, and knowing how to craft it with intention is something most leaders are not fluent in.

Today is always the best day to go deeper into defining and creating the environment you and your people crave. Every day that you wait to create an intentional culture is another day of being unintentional at best and toxic at worst.

We have all been there before: working for a company where we felt so in sync and so energized by the people and work at hand. And we know the opposite of that: working at a company that feels like it is sucking us dry, where the only connection we have is our shared complaints, and even gossip, about how little the place cares.

The Facts about Culture

Those feel-good workplaces are more than just temporary happiness. Intentional and protected environments have a direct effect on employee engagement, retention, productivity, loyalty, and profit. Thank goodness there's finally research to back all that up; it's been proven that a good culture is directly connected to a sustainable business. Take, for example, these findings:

- Businesses with a strong learning culture enjoy employee engagement and retention rates around 30 to 50 percent higher than those that don't (Robert Half).[2]

- When organizations have a thriving culture, employees rate their satisfaction with employee experience 102 percent higher (O. C. Tanner).[3]

- Thriving cultures with a positive employee experience are eight times more likely to have high incidences of great work, thirteen times more likely to have highly engaged employees, three times less likely to have layoffs, two times more likely to have an increase in revenue, three times less likely to have employees experiencing moderate to severe

---

2   Robert Half, "Employers Fear 4.5m Workers Could Be on the Move This Year," April 12, 2018, https://www.roberthalf.co.uk/press/employers-fear-45m-workers-could-be-move-year.
3   O. C. Tanner Institute, "2020 Global Culture Report," accessed April 30, 2021, https://www.octanner.com/content/dam/oc-tanner/documents/white-papers/2019/INT-GCR2020-12.pdf. All references to O.C. Tanner pertain to this report.

burnout, and seven times more likely to have employees innovating (O. C. Tanner).

- Companies with strong cultures saw a fourfold increase in revenue growth (*Forbes*).[4]

- Being named a Best Place to Work is associated with a 0.75 percent stock jump (Glassdoor).[5]

- Seventy-seven percent of employees agree that a strong culture allows them to do their best work; 76 percent see the impact in—and another 74 percent draw a correlation between—culture and their ability to serve their customer base (Eagle Hill).[6]

When culture isn't working, neither is your business:

- Toxic workplace cultures have driven 20 percent of US employees out of their jobs in the past five years, at a turnover cost greater than $223 billion (SHRM).[7]

---

4 Kotter, "Does Corporate Culture Drive Financial Performance?" *Forbes*, February 10, 2011, https://www.forbes.com/sites/johnkotter/2011/02/10/does-corporate-culture-drive-financial-performance/?sh=33b69a137e9e.

5 Andrew Chamberlain, "Does Company Culture Pay Off? Analyzing Stock Performance of 'Best Places to Work' Companies," Glassdoor, March 11, 2015, https://www.glassdoor.com/research/does-company-culture-pay-off-analyzing-stock-performance-of-best-places-to-work-companies/#.

6 Eagle Hill Consulting, "The Business Case for Culture," 2018, https://www.eaglehillconsulting.com/wp-content/uploads/Eagle-Hill-Consulting-Business-Case-For-Culture.pdf.

7 Beth Mirza, "Toxic Workplace Cultures Hurt Workers and Company Profits," Society for Human Resource Management (SHRM), September 25, 2019, https://www.shrm.org/resourcesandtools/hr-topics/employee-relations/pages/toxic-workplace-culture-report.aspx.

- Poor workplace cultures lead to a 157 percent increase in the incidence rate of moderate to severe burnout (O. C. Tanner).

- An estimated 120,000 deaths and $190 billion in health-care spending per year are attributed to employee burnout (O. C. Tanner).

- Companies with moderate-to-severe burnout have a 376 percent decrease in the odds of having highly engaged employees, an 87 percent decrease in the likelihood of employees staying, and a 22 percent decrease in work output (O. C. Tanner).

- Employees who say that they very often or always experience burnout at work are 63 percent more likely to take a sick day, 23 percent more likely to visit the emergency room, 2.6 times as likely to leave their current employer, and 13 percent less confident in their performance (O. C. Tanner).

- Disengaged employees can cost companies up to $550 billion a year (O. C. Tanner).

Toxic environments, therefore, represent more than just temporary pain. Ongoing exposure to negative people and places has the opposite effect of feel-good environments—your company's employee engagement, retention, productivity, loyalty, and profit are proven to suffer. And the part that's so tough is that you can build a really intentional and positive environment for years and then one toxic person can make the whole thing come crashing down.

The expression that "one bad apple spoils the bunch" is unfortunately true without the appropriate communication, boundaries, trust, and respect to properly manage the person's impact. But it is very possible to recover from a breakdown in your workplace culture when you know where, how, and why it happened and when you have your values to guide you back to a place of authentic alignment.

We live in a time that can now measure, quantify, and build a powerful case for why workplace culture matters (see chapters 7 and 8). And it's so incredible how much we've evolved as a society and a human race—we now realize that we can and should do better for our people.

The History of the Workweek in the United States

Let's take a walk down a historical lane for a moment...

The makings of the forty-hour workweek started in the nineteenth century. The following is a timeline of the key dates that led to the work standards we're familiar with today:

> 1817: After the Industrial Revolution, activists and labor union groups advocated for better working conditions. People were working eighty- to one-hundred-hour weeks.

> 1869: President Ulysses S. Grant issued a proclamation to guarantee eight-hour workdays for government employees. Grant's decision encouraged private-sector workers to push for the same rights.

> 1926: Henry Ford popularized the forty-hour workweek after he discovered through his research that

working more than that yielded only a small increase in productivity that lasted a short period of time.

1938: Congress passed the Fair Labor Standards Act, which required employers to pay overtime to all employees who worked more than forty-four hours a week.[8]

So it was in 1926 (nearly one hundred years ago!) that the forty-hour workweek was created. During the Industrial Revolution, eight-hour workdays were unheard of because factories typically ran around the clock. It was commonplace that employees worked ten to sixteen hours a day. Ford made a groundbreaking change by being one of the first significant company owners to shift his work policy to forty-hour weeks and five working days, with no change in wages.

However, the industrialist did not do it for his employees' comfort or to safeguard their health. His concerns were more capital oriented. Ford realized that if companies were to make a profit, customers needed to buy things, and in order to want to go shopping, customers needed to relax and enjoy themselves. For this, they needed more time off work.[9]

I was reflecting on this with my grandfather when he was in his early nineties. He started his career as an engineer in the 1940s and worked in a lot of plants that involved heavy machinery and

8 Sophie Lee, "40-Hour Work Week: The History and Evolution," Culture Amp, accessed September 9, 2020, https://explore.cultureamp.com/c/40-hour-work-week-th?x=MdEi_K.

9 *India Today* Web Desk, "Henry Ford Started the 40-Hour Workweek but the Reason Will Surprise You," *India Today*, July 27, 2017, https://www.indiatoday.in/education-today/gk-current-affairs/story/40-hour-workweek-henry-ford-1026067-2017-07-27.

chemicals. People were working around the clock, and he was part of the team that oversaw a great deal of the plant's success.

He told me that there was a protocol in place when someone made a deadly error and got physically caught in a machine: They would stop the line and get the person out, and once it was cleaned up, they'd all just move on and get back to work as if someone had spilled a cup of coffee. This was after the Fair Labor Standards Act was passed, which, although a positive move, clearly did not account for the inner workings of our humanity. Companies like my grandfather's were just fine and not even called out for operating with such flippancy of response to workers' rights, well-being, and the human experience.

In some ways I was mortified when I heard this story, and in others I was grateful. I was mortified that we'd ever lived in a world that counted deadly errors as simply issues with production. And I was grateful that we are now living in a society in which, if someone died on the job, there would likely be access to mental health support to process grief, anxiety, and stress as well as technical support for more advanced safety protocols to ensure that these grave issues never occurred again.

The Future of Work in the United States

According to the US Census, in this country 90 percent of workers were farmers in 1790; less than 2 percent are today. In just that statistic alone, we can see that we've moved significantly out of manual work and toward more mental and emotional work. And pretty soon the majority of our manual jobs will be taken over by artificial intelligence, robots, and automation.

It's predicted that up to 45 percent of jobs today will be automated out of existence in only twenty years, and twenty million manufacturing jobs globally will be replaced in the next ten years.

It is also estimated that, globally, between four hundred million and eight hundred million individuals could be displaced by automation and need to find new jobs by 2030.[10]

To many that may seem scary; to me that seems like a transformative evolution! The more that artificial intelligence takes over mundane tasks, the greater possibility there is for us humans to let go of work that doesn't require our mind, heart, and spirit to be activated. And that's the thing—AI may be able to model our minds, but it cannot take on the qualities of our heart and spirit. So those are the greatest muscles to strengthen alongside our minds.

Don't get me wrong—there are plenty of manual labor careers that are purpose driven and incredibly fulfilling. This is by no means a knock on certain jobs or looking down on work that can be replaced by a robot. Personally, I am on a quest to follow in my great uncle's footsteps and become a woodworking cowgirl. My vision is to open a retreat center in the mountains of Idaho while building furniture and art with my hands and helping to work the range on horseback with my cattlemen community out there. Every time I take on that type of physical work, I end my day with complete contentment, gratitude, and desire for more. I imagine that's how many people are when it comes to seeing the fruits of their physical labor. It all depends on the individual and the environment they have to either survive or thrive in. In other words: the quality of their culture.

Some cultures will prioritize transferable skills and development for their team members who will be faced with AI

---

10   James Manyika, Susan Lund, Michael Chui, Jacques Bughin, Jonathan Woetzel, Parul Batra, Ryan Ko, and Saurabh Sanghvi, "Jobs Lost, Jobs Gained: What the Future of Work Will Mean for Jobs, Skills, and Wages," McKinsey Global Institute, November 28, 2017, https://www.mckinsey.com/featured-insights/future-of-work/jobs-lost-jobs-gained-what-the-future-of-work-will-mean-for-jobs-skills-and-wages.

replacements. Others will let an entire team go at the drop of a hat to save a few dollars. Some cultures will intentionally plan for outsourced AI support while others will go out of business for not considering it. Some cultures will double down on their investments in human skills while others will pretend that they are consequential, losing potentially their greatest differentiator.

Just a few years ago, I hired my first administrative assistant, who books, confirms, and reschedules all my appointments. And guess what? She's a robot! I was skeptical at first, but after witnessing the precision, accuracy, and consistency of "her" support each month, it was apparent that my investment in that intelligence was more cost effective and simpler than if I had hired a human. What pushed me over the top was when my grandfather died and I reached out to my AI assistant, Clara, to tell her that I needed all my meetings postponed for the week and to let them know that I had a death in my family. Within an hour, everything had been rescheduled and I was receiving condolences from the people whose meetings with me were affected. It was a moment of realizing how dynamic and reliable my AI was. Could a human have done it? Absolutely. But did I need a human to do it? Absolutely not.

So this is where we're going: all the work that doesn't require emotional intelligence will be outsourced, and everyone who decided that emotional intelligence was just some hippie-dippie thing will be left behind in a big way.

We are evolving for the better. We are shedding the layers of what does not serve us as a human species and stepping into a greater possibility for tomorrow.

With all that evolution, there are some things that have never changed and will never change. As human beings, we are wired to crave a sense of purpose, connection, and belonging. There is no new software or latest gadget that is going to replace that.

Perhaps it can enhance it, but it can never replace it. We feel it on a cellular level, and we know in our hearts and souls when it is real. There is no substitute for these human needs in creating a meaningful life.

Attaining a sense of purpose, connection, and belonging can feel incredibly daunting and overwhelming for most people—*most people!* So many leaders feel lost when it comes to emotional intelligence. There are myriad methods, theories, and tools to choose from in developing your emotional intelligence repertoire. I encourage you to keep exploring them until you discover what unshakably resonates with you.

The Lens of Our Values

The lens through which we'll analyze the workplace—the lens of values, what uniquely matters most to us—is simple yet multifaceted.

We'll take these seemingly daunting experiences and ground them in a language you're already fluent in; you just don't know it yet. I'm referring, as you might have guessed, to the language of your values.

When you know, own, and live your values each day, you have both the direction and the boundaries for creating a culture with intention. The intensity around what to do first and where to go next will slowly fade away because you will harness your values to answer those questions.

And when you do that, you'll have the know-how to hire, engage, and retain your people through authentic actions and protocols. You'll even develop a whole team of culture keepers (see chapter 3) who will all know what's expected and required to hold themselves and others lovingly accountable to the values that connect you to one another and to the vision and mission at hand.

Permission to be human. When I use the phrase "lovingly accountable," I'm really talking about having compassion toward the person being held accountable, knowing that you, too, have needed support to do better in the past. True compassion comes about when we suspend judgment and instead ignite love. This is an accountability that is not about punitive correction according to hard-and-fast rules but rather about incorporating mutual accountability into the success of a values-driven workplace.

Whether you were someone who was inspired by your parents' or caregiver's relationship to work or someone who felt scared of it, we all have a long list of lifetime experiences that shaped our perception of what work is meant to be. And that perception is tied to the energy we expect to receive in exchange for our commitment to work. When you unlock the language of values, you'll be able to translate the ebbs and flows of your energy into an understanding of how this energy reflects or takes away from your values system.

As you know, workplace culture has a massive impact on the success of both the organization at large and the individuals who work there. There are healthy, thriving offices, and there are toxic, suffocating ones. You get to choose which environment you want to be a part of and intentionally craft around you. As you will read, there is a massive amount of data that points to how important this work is, especially amid the rise of artificial intelligence. Now is the time to decide what you and your company stand for so that you can create an environment that reflects your shared core values and the energy correlated with them.

My hope is that this book will give you a deeper understanding of the values that drive you and your people so that you can understand the environments that are being created as a result. This lens will give you a framework in which to guide and align your team's culture.

As you go through the book, you'll gain the confidence and tools you need to create a thriving workplace culture by knowing, owning, and living your values. I'll meet you where you are and guide you through a practical and replicable step-by-step process.

Values Alignment Review

1. Energy introduces itself before anyone speaks. We feel it through gut instincts, intuition, and vibes.

2. As humans, we are all walking, talking, living, breathing sets of values. And so is your company.

3. Values serve as a handshake between you and your employees on what you should expect from each other. They represent the core of the company and how you define success and failure.

4. Culture exists whether you do something about it or not. An external consultant cannot "fix" it for you.

5. Ongoing exposure to negative people and places is proven to have harmful effects on your company's engagement, retention, productivity, loyalty, and profit.

CHAPTER 2

Being a Human at Work

We don't see things as they are, we see them as we are.
—Anaïs Nin

As I shared in the introduction, before I started my company, I designed and implemented a global best practice model for young-professional engagement with one of the largest nonprofits in the world. At the time, it was the most gratifying leadership opportunity I had ever had, guiding the efforts at a local chapter of a worldwide nonprofit. I felt like I had made it.

From the beginning of my experience at the company, I had a strong internal feeling that this young-professional program was the biggest opportunity that existed for me and the community at large. I knew it would take only some intentional small tweaks to make a big impact—igniting a movement the organization had never seen before.

When I inherited the program, there was great marketing collateral but little direction, leadership, or engagement. I was empowered to do what I thought was best to shift the work from surviving to thriving.

That process started by meeting one-on-one with every volunteer who was on the board. I asked them all the same questions:

1. Why did you get involved?

2. Why have you stayed?

3. What has worked?

4. What needs to change?

5. Which of your gifts would you like to use to grow the program?

What I quickly learned was that no one had asked the board members what their interests, passions, and talents were, let alone how they could activate those things in order to expand and grow the work. Instead, they were told what was happening (or sometimes left in the dark) and expected to just show up without buy-in, perspective, or active support for the efforts at hand. They mostly felt like they were just a "butt in a seat" when it came to their engagement; even worse, most of them were volun*told* (you know, when you're expected to volunteer because your boss said so) to be there. Now for the first time, they felt like their opinions mattered, and they wanted to get reengaged in seeing what might be possible.

Permission to be human. Relatedly, there's a big difference between spitballing a bunch of questions and more of an interview style. The energy in which you approach the conversation and the way you choose to engage with curiosity sets the tone for how others will receive you. When you ask people to share vulnerably (as I did in the five questions previously listed), you must hold that information sacred. In order for something to be sacred, that person must trust you with it.

I learned from Stephen Covey in *The Speed of Trust* that in all our relationships, we have an "emotional bank account" and our interactions either increase or decrease the balance of trust and connection.[11] Every time someone keeps their word, holds your information in confidence, or follows through on their intentions, trust deposits are made. And whenever that same person says something and doesn't follow through, shares your confidential information, or breaks a promise, big withdrawals are made. The thing about this trust bank is that once a person's account is on empty (or even overdrawn), that relationship is likely toast.

Although many of these volunteers met me with very few deposits in their trust bank from the nonprofit, I was able to make a large investment on behalf of the organization by simply listening with intention and quickly following through when I heard the spark of their leadership being reignited; they were ready to make good things happen. It was remarkable how clear it was when you really boiled it down to the human experience of creating trust and empowerment. Within the initial meeting, volunteers said things like this: "Thank you for caring about my opinion. I hadn't been asked for it before." "I appreciate you taking the time to get to know me. I didn't think I mattered to this group." "I was going to leave but thought I'd give it one last chance. Thanks for helping me understand the vision here now." "I'm ready to be engaged!" "I am going to be honest with you. My CEO told me I needed to be a part of this, and I've been phoning it in. I have a ton on my plate right now and know I won't be able to commit to what you're looking for. Is there another way I can be a part of it?" Holding

---

11 Stephen Covey, *The Speed of Trust: The One Thing That Changes Everything* (New York: Free Press, 2006).

honest, psychologically safe, and vulnerable spaces from day one opened up a totally new account within their trust bank, and the balance was abundant.

As I've mentioned, based on the ballooning membership that followed, six months later my approach was named a best practice model for young-professional engagement globally.

Before all this, I figured that most leaders and organizations treated people the way they wanted to be treated, led by example, and empowered others along the way. Aren't those the typical catchphrases everyone talks about?

Yet what I know wholeheartedly now is that most people can understand business models, programs, and leadership from a nuts-and-bolts perspective, but what's not so easy to understand is the human side of it all. Whoever created the term *soft skills* to describe personality traits and behaviors wasn't taking into account how difficult these skills are for most people to master. More people are beginning to refer to soft skills as people skills or power skills. I look forward to that transition in our vernacular.

Call after call, meeting after meeting, presentation after presentation, training after training, I kept getting the same questions:

- How do you get people involved?

- How do you get them to stay?

- How do you get them to understand our work?

- How do you increase membership?

- How are you able to have them become leaders within the program?

After coaching, consulting, facilitating workshops, and giving speeches to people based on this set of questions, I found that there was a serious generational divide in knowledge of how to intentionally craft a culture that attracted and retained young professionals.

That divide was apparent when discussing the nuances of creating culture through shared values, mutually beneficial experiences, accountability, and empowerment. In the eyes of those more established in their careers, my work was considered innovative and earned me distinguished awards. In the eyes of my peers, my work was fun and intuitive—a refreshing change from their normal grind.

The insights I gained firsthand into the issues of attraction and retention were later backed up by data when I founded SparkVision and we launched our High Achieving Millennial Research Project, which we created to capture the values, characteristics, and workplace culture preferences of those born between 1980 and 2000 who are on point professionally, striving to be better, and inspiring those around them. These are people who defy the commonly accepted negative stereotypes of being overly coddled or entitled or who expect to run the place without putting in their dues.

Although most reporting on this generation focuses on quick fixes that help attract new talent, we centered our lens on the core values that underlie motivations and behaviors. When the standard fixes of remote working policies and casual dress codes failed to retain young professionals, we sought to understand the cultural norms that created the turnover. Furthermore, we aimed to understand how stress is triggered and explored avenues where it might be reduced.

Our battle cry was to stand up against those voices that have decried the "laziness" and "entitlement" of the millennial generation while paying particular attention to individuals who we have identified to be "high achieving." These high achievers were people who maintained high standards, associated achievement with competence, and took responsibility for their mistakes. They were also intrinsically motivated, recognized by colleagues as proactive self-starters, and able to find purpose in pursuing a task. Further, they often earned promotions, awards, and higher degrees; undertook extracurricular activities; and led a team or company. Every participant we recruited for this study was filtered through a formalized vetting process. Our findings are focused on millennials who employers desperately want to hire but often struggle to keep.

We humanized the millennial experience through qualitative and quantitative data that paints a more accurate picture of what High Achieving Millennials need in the workplace to thrive. Our goal was to have one thousand eligible participants take part in the research within three months. We knew we needed help.

During a launch party that rolled out this message, we created an Ambassador Program to broaden our reach and help us recruit participants for our research. Primarily millennials themselves, ambassadors used their social capital to rally for the need to understand the generation better. They actively encouraged others within their networks and organizations to contribute to our data pool. Our goal was to gain five solid ambassadors, and we got thirty to sign up that very night!

Without their dedicated advocacy, we would not have been able to provide the insights we did. It was yet another example of the proven model that ignites exponential power when we come together through our shared values to make good things happen.

In the end, we had over one thousand participants take an eighty-question survey, with no incentive or rewards, in a matter of one week. We decided to keep going and ended up with nearly three thousand national participants. In short, with the support of new team members unified through shared vision, mission, and values, we tripled our goal with ease and grace. Clearly, young professionals were eager to be painted in what felt like a more accurate light.

We had quite a few interesting findings, including the following:

- The majority (69 percent) said that their upbringing played a large role in instilling values that led to their personal success today, including work ethic, independence, perseverance, helping others, gratitude, and growth.

- The top five areas of workplace culture that mattered to respondents were accountability, opportunity for growth, positive staff relationships, direct communication, and feedback.

- Positive staff relationships were the number one reason a person stayed in their role.

- Nearly all participants (81 percent) felt the greatest sense of satisfaction when they had a sense of purpose.

- The top three things that they needed to feel satisfied were meaningful experiences, work-life balance, and connection to others (with reputation, network, income, and title all falling below).

- Over half (53 percent) had the lowest job satisfaction when transparent communication from leadership was a challenge.

It was a fascinating journey in data that illuminated something I began to realize before I started. I learned that although each generation is uniquely affected by what's going on in the world when they enter it, we have a lot more in common than we realize. I also learned that although High Achieving Millennials wanted accountability, opportunity for growth, positive staff relationships, direct communication, and feedback, so did Gen Z, Gen X, boomers, and even traditionalists. It wasn't so much a millennial thing as it was a human thing.

The biggest difference was that millennials were not willing to compromise or keep quiet about old norms that don't work. En masse, they were not willing to suck it up and clock in to work for the weekend. They are going to seek out a culture that fits their values, even if that means job hopping until they find it. And it's already shaken up the way CEOs think about how they can sustainably attract and retain worthy talent.

In the end, most humans want the same things: to feel connection, to use their gifts, to make a difference, to be heard and understood, and to know that their voice matters. When we engage people in a culture where those pieces are being fulfilled, that's when real power is ignited.

Form Tribes, not Groups

When I read Seth Godin's book *Tribes*, light bulbs turned on left and right.[12] The young-professionals program I was running generated such significant and measurable results because we weren't just another group—*we were a tribe!* And we all grew stronger together because of it.

---

12 Seth Godin, *Tribes: We Need You to Lead Us* (New York: Penguin Group, 2008).

Here is what I gleaned are the key differences between the two:

Group	Tribe
A number of people	A community of people
Expectation drives participation	Purpose drives participation
Undefined values and inconsistent culture	Clearly defined values and aligned culture
Propelled by manager's task list	Propelled by leader's vision
Members are told what to do	Members are empowered to use their gifts
Often lack trust and communication	Are grounded in trust and communication
About stuff	About connection
Don't tend to know one another	Respect and care for one another

Looking at each of these statements, on which side does your team lean? Are you heavy on the group norms and light on the tribe? Perhaps you have a mix, or perhaps it's pretty clear cut.

Permission to be human. Wherever you are, meet yourself there without judgment. Have gratitude for what's working and for the awareness of where there's opportunity to evolve. This isn't about having all the boxes checked. It's about consciously evolving into the norm that best serves your people. This book will serve you in the journey from a group to a tribe.

I have the immense pleasure today of being the values guide for leaders and their organizations, transforming their groups into tribes. It's always different and it's always the same. That's because it always involves humans. When people are connected through their values, there's no limit to what they can do. Values-driven tribes create a culture in which talent is fostered and new meaning is brought into each person's life.

If you could do that in your company, wouldn't you think it was worth a try?

Fixing the Floor

Don't get me wrong—this is far from a rainbows-and-sunshine path. Even while I was leading that astonishing tribe, I had days when I didn't want to get out of bed and deal with the people who were on the peripheries of the work. I would often feel totally overwhelmed by everything that I needed to do to get the results I desired in a way that aligned with my values. I had pressure from my internal leadership to take an easier path. The problem was that the solution they had in mind went against my values.

I remember a one-on-one in which my boss said, "You just have to lower the bar. Your expectations are too high, and it's making other people look bad." Another time I was told, "It's not appropriate for you to share information about what's on the horizon. Just because you know it's coming doesn't mean you have to tell your team that."

The "coaching" I was receiving often left me feeling sick. And because at the time I was still living in a people-pleasing mindset where I made myself smaller to make others more comfortable, I took their feedback to be true instead of questioning its intentions. I didn't put it through my own filter to determine whether I was going to accept that truth or ground myself in my own.

I'll never forget the advice I received when I asked a trusted colleague if they thought I was wrong for sharing my vision of the future—what was in place and what needed to be created. He looked at me with so much empathy in his eyes and shared a story: "I want you to imagine that you physically came into this company for the first time and you noticed that the floor wasn't level. In fact, it was on such an angle that people were getting back problems, and things were sliding around and even getting lost. You noticed this for a couple of days, and you finally got the courage to speak up. You said something to your colleagues like, 'Hey, did you ever notice that we're losing things and our backs are hurting because the floor is so uneven? Is there something we can do to change that?' and they responded, 'Oh yeah, but it's not that bad. You just have to start walking on an angle, and it will feel like it's evened out. Just bend over a little more, and you'll get used to it.'"

He went on: "That's what's going on here now. You are trying to fix the floor, and everyone else is just comfortable in the pain of it. They don't care if they lose things or their backs hurt because this is what they know and what they protect. It's a lot of work to pull up the entire foundation and rebuild what's broken. But you're the kind of person who wants to do that work. And we need more people like that to speak up about the floor and not be afraid of the consequences."

I just about cried when he used that analogy. He was right. I had no interest in bending over, experiencing pain, and losing things when it was obvious what needed to be done to fix it.

I resigned within a few days of that conversation, realizing over and over again that I wanted to build my own floor and help those who were interested in building theirs with intention from the start, or those who were willing to rip up the whole damn thing to do what was right to ensure that they were working from the same, solid level.

Humans with Human Issues

I've now worked with companies from just about every sector: construction, health care, education, nonprofits, start-ups, tech, consultants, security, entertainment, manufacturing, and energy, to name a few. The thing that's universal about all these diverse organizations is that they all work with and for *humans*.

And when you're working with humans, there will naturally be human issues: people not getting on board with your big vision, people choosing to gossip about issues instead of address them, people who will take their bad day out on anyone in their path, people who care more about the bottom line than how it impacts the well-being of their teams. People who don't know how to give constructive feedback from a place of kindness or at all. People who choose to give their power away instead of voicing their opinions. People who are scared of what might happen to them if they say anything other than what they've been prescribed. People who have no idea how to motivate others from a place of empowerment versus pain. People who are hurting and don't know how to help themselves out instead of projecting their hurt onto others. So where do you start?

Psychological Safety, Vulnerability, and a Sense of Purpose

According to Daniel Coyle's research in *The Culture Code*, humans across all sectors of organizations are looking for three things: psychological safety, the ability to be vulnerable (which is connected to that very safety), and a sense of purpose.[13] These three things are paramount to being able to attempt any of this work. And they all begin with psychological safety, which is defined as people's perceptions of the consequences of taking interpersonal risks in a particular context, such as a workplace.[14]

Think about it—how can you have difficult conversations with people about their behavior being out of alignment with your values if there isn't a foundation of psychological safety? That goes for both the person giving and the person receiving that coaching. It's tough to hold people accountable to things if you're afraid of their reaction.

In Adam Grant's book *Think Again*, he shared the following breakdown of what does and doesn't happen when psychological safety is at play.[15]

13 Daniel Coyle, *The Culture Code: The Secrets of Highly Successful Groups* (New York: Bantam Books, 2018).

14 Amy C. Edmondson and Zhike Lei, "Psychological Safety: The History, Renaissance, and Future of an Interpersonal Construct," *Annual Review of Organizational Psychology and Organizational Behavior* 1 (March 2014), 23–43, https://www.annualreviews.org/doi/full/10.1146/annurev-orgpsych-031413-091305.

15 Adam Grant, *Think Again: The Power of Knowing What You Don't Know* (New York: Viking, 2021), 210.

Psychological Safety at a Glance

When you have it:	When you don't have it:
See mistakes as opportunities to learn	See mistakes as threats to your career
Willing to take risks and fail	Unwilling to rock the boat
Speaking your mind in meetings	Keeping your ideas to yourself
Openly sharing your struggles	Only touting your strengths
Trust in your teammates and supervisors	Fear of teammates and supervisors
Sticking your neck out	Having it chopped off

I once worked for a boss who would listen in on my phone calls when I was talking to clients or prospects. She never asked me whether this was OK or even let me know she was going to do it. But I could hear the line click over (this was back in the days when landlines were the norm at work), and she'd promptly come to my office afterward and educate me on where I had gone wrong in my conversation. I once even noticed her listen in on the line when I was having a personal conversation with my aunt. Apparently, I was on the line too long, and that was her way of making it known.

Can you imagine what an enormous lack of psychological safety that created? In an office of three, I felt like I was being stalked. It's unsurprising that her bad behavior wasn't limited to just calls. She was constantly getting in fights with her mother (the former founder of the organization) and her husband—loud enough for the whole office to hear. Mandatory team lunches together typically included gossiping about former employees.

The trust bank withdrawals were huge; I was overdrawn from the account I shared with her. Looking back, I understand this as a classic example of a trend: it's typically not an issue of just one value being out of alignment but rather misalignments in a whole bunch of values whose integrity would have been necessary to transform that environment into a thriving culture.

When I finally quit that job, it felt like I had gotten out of a burning building before it took me down with it. My head was really messed up from the intensity of the energetic toxins that seeped into my pores there each day. I thought that I must have been such a loser to be trapped in such a place. Like I wasn't worthy of anything better because it was already so hard to just find this job. I was defeated, depleted, and all over unwell. It was like I was taking a daily double dose of crazy pills. And without the foundation of being able to feel like it was safe to simply be me, there was little to no room for my personal recovery by staying in that role.

I learned over and over again what it felt like to be in a culture that was disconnected from my values. It gave me extraordinary information to understand how potent it is to create and collaborate with others in an environment in which it feels safe to speak your truth, safe to share authentically and vulnerably, and safe to express joy for the sense of purpose you have in your work.

At the same time, let's not take for granted the power and meaning in our low points. We can choose to be mindful seekers of the exact workplace environment that's right for our intrinsic motivators. Learning what it isn't is just as important as leaning what it is. When you embrace the suck, you can pick up the gems that lie in the wisdom of your wounds and make choices that align with your values to not make the same mistakes again. Especially if you're at the helm of creating that culture.

Permission to be human. Not everyone wants to have team lunches, and for others that could be the highlight of the role. Not everyone wants to be innovative all the time; some prefer routine and efficiency. Not everyone wants to go out for happy hour with colleagues; they would prefer to get home early to be with family. What's key to understand is that none of these are the "ideal." The ideal is what is a reflection of *your values*—not what society or other organizations like yours are doing.

Harmonious cultures can exist where people can both eat alone and with their teams, innovate in small spurts and keep things running as is the rest of the time, and go out for happy hour without FOMO (fear of missing out) because they know that being with family is the most important thing of all. Often it's just a matter of the subculture of a specific team or a leadership style that will make or break your experience and vision for the culture that works for you.

One of my first coaching clients was a government executive who had recently been promoted to lead a team, a role that was far outside of her comfort or happy zone. In our first session, she asked me if I was going to change her into an extrovert. It broke my heart on the spot, and I asked, "Why would you think that?" She went on: "Because that's the ideal type of leader, but that's really not who I am." I met her there to tell her that my goal was to help her become more of who she was inside, more of who she feels the most aligned with, and more of her most authentic being. To ask her to put on a mask or muscle through changing her personality to suit others would have been straight-up regressive. The goal was to have her create a culture that worked for who she is and that the team appreciated, not for what other people were like.

Permission to be human. When you can create a sense of belonging within yourself through psychological safety, vulnerability, and purpose by being who you are, you subconsciously are giving others permission to be the same—and you can't genuinely create that with others if you don't have it with yourself first. I had a significant lesson in that very concept.

After being inducted into the *Daily Record*'s Circle of Excellence (meaning I had won the recognition of the top one hundred women in the state of Maryland three times), I saved my application responses. I did that for the first time because I thought there was no way in hell that I would have won this after what I wrote under my "greatest professional accomplishment" section. When I truly looked deeply at what I was most proud of, it was bigger than my fancy client names, business growth, or even the quality of work I was offering. I shared that "my greatest professional accomplishment is that I get to wake up every day, exactly as I am, offer my gifts, and build a life that is an expression of my values, beliefs, and authentic self." And after expanding on that, I became the youngest—and fastest—recipient of this honor.

Now I teach an entire workshop for people who desire similar recognition but who have not yet learned how to own their power through their personal hero(ine)'s journey. When I shared the story of what I wrote to win my award, masses of people reached out to thank me for reminding them that being themselves, and not doing it through puffing out their chests or beating on drums they didn't care about, was a huge accomplishment. Attendees shared that they wanted that for themselves, and they were eager to go on their own journey to discover their authentic alignment with who they were at their core.

This reminds me of two profound quotes. Maya Angelou said, "I don't trust people who don't love themselves and tell me, 'I love you.'" Relatedly, Glennon Doyle said, "I have stopped asking people for directions to places they've never been." Let those sink in for a moment.

If you really want to get into creating a values-driven, thriving workplace culture, start within yourself. What do you need to do to heal so that you don't bleed on people who didn't cut you? What baggage are you carrying around that is getting in your way of having a sense of purpose, vulnerability, or psychological safety with yourself?

This book is not designed to walk you through that, but I'd encourage you to find a teacher, a coach, a therapist, a mentor, a healer, or even a wise and trusted loved one to start the conversation. It wasn't until I went to weekly mindfulness-based psychotherapy, coaching, and myriad healers that I was able to truly embrace my wounds and find the wisdom that lay within, enabling me to become an authentic leader today.

The Mirror

Most of us need to take a deep look in the mirror to see where we can improve ourselves before we have the integrity to ask others to improve themselves. This idea translates and flows into all aspects of our lives. Think about it. Someone who can't give constructive feedback to their team members is likely also unable to tell their best friend what would improve their relationship. Someone who can't figure out how to (or doesn't care to) empower their people at work is likely not crushing the empowerment train with their kids' chores. It's not impossible, but it's highly unlikely. And the biggest shame of all of is that very few of us are ever taught these skills, especially from a place where the teacher holds us lovingly accountable and helps us back up when we fall flat on our faces.

Difficult conversations are just that—difficult. One go at them is not enough to build that muscle. It takes trying over and over and over again until you gain the confidence, skills, and wisdom to get it. The only real teacher is life itself. And we can only do the deep, transformative work when it's happening.

How many people wind up getting divorced because it seems easier than talking about and exploring the issues between them? How many people ghost out on a job because they'd rather burn a bridge than have a confrontation about leaving? How many people suffer silently as a victim of their surroundings instead of making the choice to change the view?

We like to pretend that there's a line between work and life (the whole balance thing), but it's really just life. And when we can focus in on and build these human skills, our lives overall are immeasurably better—plain and simple.

So let's choose to fix the floor instead of bending over. When we speak up about it, it shows other people that they can too. It's miraculous what permission we give to others when we're true to ourselves.

The work of creating a thriving culture, and therefore a business, is not for people looking for a quick fix or who believe that this is a one-and-done approach. Culture exists every day, whether you're intentional about it or not.

If you want to get in better physical health, you can sign up for the quick weight loss infomercial plan and bounce back to your old habits as soon as the New Year's guilt passes. Or you can really look at your lifestyle and see where you're able to make small, intentional shifts to create a state of general well-being. Eating salad for a week, taking one vitamin, stretching one afternoon, or lifting weights for one hour is not going to change your overall physical state. You have to do those things consistently forever. There is no shortcut for sustainable change. And the same goes for culture. One powerful retreat, one afternoon of deep conversations, or one well-known motivational speaker is just a quick hit of possibility, not a sustainable approach to each day.

We must be intentional about knowing the balance on our trust banks with one another at work—by holding honest, psychologically safe, and vulnerable conversations. To do that, we must make a commitment to developing our emotional intelligence skills and truly caring about those soft skills just as much (if not more) than the hard skills. No matter what generation you're a part of, people will appreciate your effort and attention to your personal embodiment of your inner work and the values associated with it. You must start within yourself if you want others to follow. Once you do, you are giving others permission to be the same. There's no shortcut for this work, but there is a path I will lead you on, and we will take it one step at a time, without judgment of pace.

Here's your chance to bail out or step up.

This book is *not* for those who are

- looking for a silver bullet to solve other people's problems;

- not invested in their people and themselves; or

- hoping someone else can fix their culture for them.

This book *is* for those who are

- willing to start the deep work with themselves before they project onto others;

- deeply invested in their people and themselves; and

- interested in learning through the discomfort of growth.

So are we cool to keep going together?

Values Alignment Review

1. We have an "emotional bank account," and our interactions either increase or decrease the balance of trust and connection.

2. It's not so much a millennial thing as it is a human thing.

3. Humans crave psychological safety, vulnerability, and a sense of purpose.

4. Start within yourself if you want to create a values-driven, thriving workplace culture.

5. There is no shortcut for sustainable change in culture.

CHAPTER 3

How Values and Behaviors Create Culture

We want leaders who practice their values, not just profess them.
We want courage—not slogans on posters. Speak up, listen,
and be brave.

—Brené Brown

'll repeat: As human beings, we're walking, talking, living, breathing sets of values. And so is your company. It's that clear and that opaque all at once. So what are values anyway?

Values are intrinsic motivators that represent a person's principles or standards of behavior—one's judgment of what is important in life. Your core values are as unique as your fingerprints. They serve as your internal compass and represent what you stand for. When you honor your values, life feels good. And when you don't, your mental, emotional, and physical states suffer. The things that make your heart flutter and the things that make your stomach ache are often reflections of whether an experience is aligned with your values. Happiness is impossible if you abandon your values.

Common values include things like connection, a sense of belonging, purpose, true friendship, family stability, and growth. There are thousands of words that can represent the things that matter most to your sense of personal alignment. In the next chapter, we'll dive into a much bigger list of values to refer to.

In the workplace, values represent the core of who you are as a company and how you define success and failure. Core values are the fundamental beliefs of a person or organization. These beliefs create standards for behavior and support people in understanding the difference between right and wrong. Core values also help companies to determine whether they are on the path to fulfilling their goals by creating an unwavering guide.

Strong values resonate among kindred spirits, those individuals who will share in the sacrifices that have to be made when things are hard. Commitment to values comes in those moments of tension when you lean on your values to move forward in a way that won't conflict with your conscience. In order for values to have an effect on driving positive behavior and decision-making, they must be clear and direct. Ideally, values should also represent what's unique about the mindset of your organization.

When I deliver keynotes, I often ask the audience to raise their hands if their company has core values. Typically about 75 percent of the room will gingerly shoot their hands up. Then I ask them to keep their hand raised if they can name their values without looking. Only a few hands stay in the air. And when I ask that person or two if they could share a story of their company values in action within the last week, I'm lucky if just one of them can do it.

Can you imagine working at a place that not only professed its values but also behaved in alignment with them every day? That did it so darn well that every employee could recall a story of something that happened *that day* that reflected those values?

I'm not just talking about big things, like whom they wound up hiring to lead a new team. I'm also talking about the little things, like someone holding the door open for you and asking you how your mom is doing, knowing she had surgery recently. It's the big, the little, and everything in between that is an expression of someone's values.

When a company is intentional about their values as it relates to whom they hire, coach, promote, and fire, they have taken tremendous steps to ensure that their culture reflects those very values they claim to hold sacred. Corporate values alignment is when your organization's stated core values are congruent with the behaviors, policies, and practices of their people and overall culture.

When true values alignment exists, every workday is filled with purpose, pride, and productivity.

The Culture Formula

Culture can feel like an overwhelming and daunting experience. When I first became a culture consultant, I often found myself in those same shoes, unsure of what to prioritize and focus on to have a true impact. Then I found a formula that simplifies all this culture stuff and will give you clarity on how to define and align your own company's culture with its values.

$$\text{Values} \times \text{Behavior} = \text{Culture}$$

I saw this formula on Simon Sinek's website and thought how much easier this made the complexities of culture.[16] Let's be clear—this formula is not an exact science. Culture does not

16 Simon Sinek, "Transform Your Culture," accessed August 30, 2018, https://simonsinek.com/transform-your-culture/.

work that way. It is not that straightforward. The formula is meant to provide a basic framework to remember and consider when you are looking at your own culture. It's not perfect, but it's a fantastic lens of analysis. Behaviors are values in action. What actions are your people taking?

Let's break it down further.

Your core values multiplied by the behaviors of your people ultimately create your culture. Let's consider the value of integrity—what behaviors could you list that were commonplace for your people as it relates to this value? Would they be in alignment with behaviors like transparent communication, ongoing accountability, or trusting relationships? Or might there be disconnected behaviors like siloed communication, lack of accountability, or ongoing unkept promises? When you can see and make note of the behaviors that are in or out of alignment with your stated core values, you can start to understand what's driving your culture for better or for worse.

Using the formula, it might translate to something like this:

$$\text{Integrity} \times \text{Transparent Communication} = \text{Intrinsically Motivated, Engaged, Reliable}$$

Or on the flip side:

$$\text{Integrity} \times \text{Lack of Communication} = \text{Insufficiently Motivated, Disconnected, Unreliable}$$

When you use this framework, it's impressive how quickly you will be able to get whether your company lives what it preaches. And that's mostly because we feel this stuff deeply. Our bodies, minds, hearts, and spirits know when we're in a good place that is true to its word or in a disconnected place that is not. Our values and behaviors are the keys to defining and showing the world what we stand for.

Vision, Mission, Values

How do values line up with your company's vision and mission?

A vision is the *why* of your company—*why* you're doing the thing you do.

The mission is the *what* of your company—*what* you do every day.

And the values are the *how* of your company—*how* you accomplish your *what* to get to your *why*.

Let's dig into that a bit more by looking at some examples before we explore the culture side of it. If you worked at the widget-making factory, it could look something like this:

- Vision: To ignite more happiness in the world through our widgets. (That's *why* you're doing it—to create more happiness.)

- Mission: To create the best widgets our customers have ever experienced. (That's *what* you're doing every day—creating the best widgets for your customers.)

- Values:
  - Empowerment: We trust our team and encourage them to use their best judgment when opportunities arise.

  - Joy: We create experiences where we have fun, celebrate, and honor happiness.

- Community: We support one another and our customers through authentic connection. (These are *how* the work is being accomplished—the behaviors that are expected to be ignited in the way the work is getting done.)

Here are those statements for my own company, SparkVision, and a few of our clients:

SparkVision

- Vision: To live in a world where we proudly embrace our truest selves to bring deeper meaning and connection to work and life.

- Mission: To create value-driven cultures where people thrive by activating their shared beliefs and motivations.

- Values:
  - Authenticity and Transparency: Be yourself—it's your greatest superpower. Take off your mask, trust your intuition, and proactively share the highs and the lows.

  - Vulnerability and Empathy: Be open. Express and expose the experiences that are too often left unsaid. Support and show love to those who have the courage to do so.

  - Accountability and Inner Harmony: Be aligned. Stay true to your positive intentions, especially with yourself. Your state of personal alignment ignites our shared success.

My Cousin's Nuts

- Vision: To fuel positive energy globally with My Cousin's Nuts all over the world.

- Mission: To create healthy, tasty, flavored nut creations that you can't wait to share with your loved ones.

- Values:
  - Authenticity: Be real. Our creations reflect our passion for the enjoyment of real food.

  - Health: Be well. We craft our products to satisfy your cravings without the junk.

  - Humor: Have fun. Life is too short to not make nut jokes.

Above and Beyond Movement

- Vision: To ignite a movement of small business owners who live in alignment and make a positive impact on the world.

- Mission: We empower small business owners using a holistic and foundational approach with a focus on mindset, team building, and client experience.

- Values:
  - Authenticity: We choose honesty with our actions and words to connect to clients with integrity.

- Growth: We tap into our expertise to create life-changing learning that takes our clients to new heights.

- Influence: We create a positive impact by empowering our clients to make meaningful contributions that have the power to ignite a movement.

Here are some examples of well-known companies' visions, missions, and values:

Johns Hopkins Medicine[17]

- Vision: Johns Hopkins Medicine pushes the boundaries of discovery, transforms health care, advances medical education, and creates hope for humanity. Together, we will deliver the promise of medicine.

- Mission: The mission of Johns Hopkins Medicine is to improve the health of the community and the world by setting the standard of excellence in medical education, research, and clinical care. Diverse and inclusive, Johns Hopkins Medicine educates medical students, scientists, health-care professionals, and the public; conducts biomedical research; and provides patient-centered medicine to prevent, diagnose, and treat human illness.

---

17 Johns Hopkins Medicine, "Johns Hopkins Medicine Mission, Vision and Values," accessed May 21, 2019, https://www.hopkinsmedicine.org/about/mission.html.

- Values:
  - Excellence and Discovery: Be the best. Commit to exceptional quality and service by encouraging curiosity, seeking information, and creating innovative solutions.

  - Leadership and Integrity: Be a role model. Inspire others to achieve their best and have the courage to do the right thing.

  - Diversity and Inclusion: Be open. Embrace and value different backgrounds, opinions, and experiences.

  - Respect and Collegiality: Be kind. Listen to, understand, and embrace others' unique skills and knowledge.

IKEA[18]

- Vision: To create a better everyday life for many people.

- Mission: To offer a wide range of well-designed, functional home furnishing products at prices so low that as many people as possible will be able to afford them.

- Values:
  - Caring for people and planet: We want to be a force for positive change. We have the possibility to make a significant and lasting impact—today and for the generations to come.

---

18 IKEA, "Vision & Business Idea," accessed June 14, 2020, https://www.ikea.com/us/en/this-is-ikea/about-ikea/vision-and-business-idea-pub9cd02291.

- Cost-consciousness: As many people as possible should be able to afford a beautiful and functional home. We constantly challenge ourselves and others to make more from less without compromising on quality.

- Simplicity: A simple, straightforward, and down-to-earth way of being is part of our Småland heritage. It is about being ourselves and staying close to reality. We are informal, pragmatic, and see bureaucracy as our biggest enemy.

- Renew and improve: We are constantly looking for new and better ways forward. Whatever we are doing today, we can do better tomorrow. Finding solutions to almost impossible challenges is part of our success and a source of inspiration to move on to the next challenge.

- Different with a meaning: IKEA is not like other companies, and we don't want to be. We like to question existing solutions, think in unconventional ways, experiment, and dare to make mistakes—always for a good reason.

- Give and take responsibility: We believe in empowering people. Giving and taking responsibility are ways to grow and develop as individuals. Trusting each other, being positive, and being forward looking inspires everyone to contribute to development.

- Lead by example: We see leadership as an action, not a position. We look for people's values before competence and experience. People who "walk the talk" and lead by example. It is about being our best self and bringing out the best in each other.

Values, Value Statements, and Guiding Principles

When it comes to uncovering the words and sentences that define your values, the experience can be exciting and daunting all at once. Having done this work for many years now, I find that a lot of teams create value statements or guiding principles instead of homing in on their true core values.

What's the difference? A core value is typically a word or term that could be found in the dictionary, such as *gratitude* or *sense of belonging*. They are typically nouns and connote a feeling or emotion.

Value statements or guiding principles are typically sentences about a certain value. They may be catchy phrases or concepts to help people remember what really matters. Using IKEA as an example, the value of responsibility is written out as a statement or guiding principle as "Give and take responsibility."

There is a distinct yet subtle difference. A value is typically one word that you could find in the dictionary. A values statement or guiding principle is a short phrase that's related to your values. Later on you'll learn about what I call value promises, which often sound like guiding principles or value statements.

Permission to be human. It doesn't *really* matter if you use one over the other; however, it would be nice if people understood the difference and classified them accordingly. Do what feels best to you and your team and own it. If you're doing this work, it's not about doing it perfectly; it's about doing it in a way that resonates with you and your team.

Get the Buy-In

Most organizations have these statements on their websites, perhaps on some posters on the walls, and maybe even in their electronic signatures. But according to Brené Brown's research, fewer than 10 percent of companies with defined values take the time to integrate them into the day-to-day practice of *how* they accomplish their work.[19]

More often than not, values were a box that was checked in order to go through the marketing and communication motions, and that's about as far as they went. Let me be clear—this is *not* a knock on branding professionals in any way. We often need help in finding these words; whoever is leading the work must engage the entire team in the process if the ultimate goal is adoption. If team members are not bought in, the values are simply bestowed on them, and they're expected to embrace them.

What if you were working at a company for decades and then out of the blue, they hired a consultant to create their vision, mission, and values, and they talked only to a select C-suite level of the team? That team comes out of the process feeling superstoked and proud of what they accomplished together. But when it comes time to share it with the greater organization at large, there are some whispers, side-eyes, and head scratching. The sentiment is "Whose company are they talking about? Those may be our aspirations, but they don't reflect who we are now."

I've seen it time and time again—the executive team puts a stake in the ground and expects everyone to get on board without engaging them in the process of understanding which stake matters most and where to put it.

Seem far-fetched? Maybe this resonates more: I once worked with a global health-care organization that spent tens of thousands

---

19 Brené Brown, *Dare to Lead: Brave Work. Tough Conversations. Whole Hearts.* (New York: Random House, 2018), 190.

of dollars on new technology for their call center. They engaged only the director of the call center and their head of tech in the process. Once they signed the contract and got the new system up and running, the call center operators were up in arms. This technology was worse than what they had before. It didn't allow them to do the basics they needed to serve their clients efficiently, and the data they had before wasn't transferable. When I sat with some of these staff members, they said, with frustration and sadness in their voices, "No one ever asked us what we thought was the most important for this upgrade. They never involved us in the conversations. And because they're not inputting this data, they couldn't have known about these glaring issues. So now we're stuck with an expensive new system that doesn't work for our needs."

This is the same type of feeling that people have when they are told or mandated to show up in one way (values), but they never agreed to it when they were brought on board and were never involved in the buy-in process.

On the flip side, what would have been possible if the program director and chief technology officer had still taken the lead on overseeing the database upgrades but, after gathering all the key information, had called a team meeting in which they presented them, asked for feedback, and encouraged people to share what would or wouldn't work for them? Often just one conversation moves "living your values" from a nice idea to a real experience.

Culture Keepers and Culture Killers

When I started my company, I found that it was harder than I realized to translate workplace culture into phrasing that was both productive and relatable. Without a doubt there is a solid learning curve separating those who get the distinct language associated with the emotional intelligence side of culture and those who do not. In other words, you either speak that language or you don't. Only those who care to build on or learn this vocabulary will be successful in the long game of culture.

After just a few weeks of being in business (and the need for my services not being clear to my audience), I knew I had to create my own terminology, one that wouldn't require a ten-minute explanation, something that would make sense no matter whom I was talking to. Enter two big players for describing people in the workforce: culture keepers and culture killers.

Without any description, you probably have a solid idea of who I'm talking about, right? Those who make you feel warm and fuzzy, and those whom you avoid like the plague. We have all experienced both—and we all know whom we prefer to surround ourselves with.

Culture keepers are the individuals who lead and maintain the positive aspects of their organization's environment, a reflection of the company's core values. They are often at the center of positive work experiences. These team members typically have high emotional intelligence. They can be new hires or lifers—tenure doesn't determine their reach. They authentically bring their personality and ideals into daily engagements. They're not perfect, so when they make mistakes, they own them and grow as a result. They don't focus only on their needs but also on what's right for the team. They're the ones who care more about their people than just about meeting a deadline. They are the ones we often want to spend time with. We want to be around them because they're always helping us to see the potential in everything.

Culture keepers are the folks who other team members look forward to collaborating with. They ask you how you are doing and really want to know the answer. They listen for when you might be struggling on a project and unconditionally jump in to help. Others often confide in them, and they can raise the bar simply from the sincerity and authenticity with which they carry themselves. This doesn't mean that all these folks are playing an extroverted cheerleader kind of role; you can do that and be a very quiet person, simply by the way you behave. Culture keepers are the ones who hold up the positive aspects of a company's daily norms. Most of the time, that is just who they are. They don't act this way because of an incentive program or special training. These are people who want to do good work and be good people while doing it.

Leadership within organizations should be working hard to nurture their culture keepers' talents and to retain them as long as possible—because they are doing so much more than just their jobs when it comes to maintaining healthy energy in their space.

Culture killers, on the other hand, are the people who are both actively and passively taking away from a positive work experience. And sadly, these folks have the power to take down a whole team of culture keepers. Companies often want to hire me to come in and "fix their culture issue" without addressing the person or the people who are creating it; they want to make a workaround. And that's not how it happens. It's like expecting someone to just learn how to be a better swimmer while having a ball and chain attached to their leg.

These culture killers are the people who always point out something that is wrong, and when new ideas arise, their response is, "Yes, but..." They are often found spreading rumors in the break room and using gossip as a form of currency. They have a bad day and think it is perfectly acceptable to take it out on others. They have little to no self-awareness, and other team members practically hide from their path so that they do not get hit by their venom. And although it is not an excuse for their actions, culture killers are the humans who are suffering—how they act on the outside reflects what they feel on the inside.

Don't be fooled: Often the biggest of the culture killers are those at the top. They have been in the organization so long that they feel they can get away with anything because they're so "needed." They can use an organization like their own game of chess and manipulate people in ways that result in the ultimate death of positivity.

Anywhere we go, we're all just balls of energy. If our energy (through body language, speech, or behavior) signals to other people that they don't belong, they're less than, what they're doing isn't meaningful, or their opinions don't matter, then we are choosing to be a culture killer. Some people feel that their way is the only way or maybe ignore you all the time, making you feel like you are never seen, heard, or listened to. Maybe the person is talking to everyone else about an issue they have with an individual instead of thoughtfully approaching people with whom they need to have hard conversations. These are all classic qualities of culture killers. Their energy kills the good vibes that were trying to survive in their workplace.

Plain and simple: Culture killers are values violators. When they're not held accountable, the values mean nothing. In the words of Perry Belcher, "Nothing will kill a great employee faster than watching you tolerate a bad one."

Your culture is only as strong as the worst behavior that is allowed, ignored, or gossiped about. If you want to truly live your values, you must be willing to terminate someone over behaviors that are out of alignment with your company's core values. Otherwise, core values are just nice ideas that have no weight. When you get to that place, your values can work against you and become a point of profound frustration and anger for your team.

You see, culture is not one size fits all. There are likely organizations that are much better equipped and designed to work with the person you need to let go of in order to protect your values. Letting someone go doesn't need to be seen as this awful result. It's helping both sides of the equation to step up more authentically regarding who they are and where they can make the biggest impact. I coached a CEO through major terminations of culture killers who were entrenched in her organization's negative cultural norms. To empower her through the process, we framed the experience as liberating the team and those two leaders from being in an environment that wasn't supporting their well-being. It was true for both sides of the equation.

I'm not suggesting that you terminate someone right off the bat. You need to give them a chance to be coached and held accountable. After they're given that guidance and the space to make new choices, if they're not on board to change and evolve, then it's time to let them go so that they can find a culture that's a better fit. It's not fair for either of you to keep suffering at that point.

If it is acceptable for someone to go around talking badly about others while remaining unwilling to talk to those people directly or to berate people instead of coaching them...that's as good as your culture is. You cannot excuse that and put blinders on because "they're really great at sales." Let me tell you, if you didn't know already: people—your people—talk about these toxic people and experiences a lot.

The play-by-play recaps of those behaviors are being relived well past when they happened. The gossip ensues and then that "isolated" experience is lived out in secondhand, thirdhand, fourth-hand, fifteenth-hand exposure in the storytelling of it. Because of our negativity bias, these stories stick harder than ones of celebration. Negativity bias is the notion that, even when of equal intensity, things of a more negative nature have a greater effect on one's psychological state and processes than neutral or positive things.

How our minds love to cling to what's wrong, bad, or a problem as opposed to what's right, good, or possible. Unfortunately, our brains are wired that way, and we have to do some serious reprogramming to change it. *You know what I'm talking about, right?* That annual review where you got high marks in every area but one, and instead of celebrating the nine positive areas, you beat yourself up for the one area you need to improve on? I used to do this a lot with feedback surveys. I'd get high marks across the board and then there would be one person who'd give me a low score and make a comment like, "She had no idea what she was talking about." Instead of celebrating the 199 positive reviews, I'd just want to know who this one person was and how I could make things right with them. Looking back, I know what a silly use of energy that was.

Know who your culture keepers and culture killers are, and work with them to cultivate more or fewer of the behaviors that are or aren't serving the energy you want to create in your workplace. At times leadership can be played, and some culture killers get away with bad behavior because leaders are blindsided or oblivious based on their firsthand experience. It's important that there are safe and confidential spaces for team members to report these experiences to gain additional support in their growth. Whether it be through your HR team or via a more informal system, be sure that people can be heard and know that what they have to say matters. Nothing is worse than someone vulnerably sharing a traumatic experience at the hands of a culture killer and having it ignored. The worst kind of pain is getting hurt by the person you explained your pain to.

I often say that a company's culture is simply its personality. These two main character types make a big impact in the overall collective personality of your team.

Here are a few qualities that lie at different ends of the spectrum:

Culture Keeper	Culture Killer
Identifies issues and presents them with solutions at hand	Complains about the situation but doesn't try to solve it
Believes in your organization's mission	Has no connection to the big picture
Optimistic about the team's future	Only cares about how the future affects them
Transparent about work experiences	Gossips about work experiences
Consistent in messaging and communication	Changes the story depending on their mood and audience
Trustworthy adviser to colleagues	Colleagues avoid them when possible
Embodies values	Violates values

Look at this list; do you know where you fall? Do you recognize the presence of these people in your organization? Could you make a list of names for both columns right now? I know that we all want to see ourselves as culture keepers and not culture killers, but it's not always that cut and dried. Although it can be nice to put people into categories, it can also be dangerous to put hard labels on them. We want to use these concepts as a starting point, not as a way to judge and box people in.

Permission to be human. We all have bad days; we all have times when our temper is shorter or we're carrying a really heavy burden in our personal lives that simply can't be cut off at work, so it seeps through. That does *not* make you a culture killer. That makes you a human. But if you're having a bad day, every day, without a break, that's another story.

If you wind up bringing up an issue from the past, that doesn't mean you're a culture killer. You need to speak the truth about obstacles; if you get stuck there and are unable to move on and are insisting that we focus on what's wrong...that's where it starts to go in a direction that we need to come back from. It's not about ignoring something or putting blinders on and saying it's not real; it's about acknowledging and consciously moving forward from that starting place.

Evolving from a Culture Killer to a Culture Keeper

You can and will be able to shift from one column to another, if you choose to. It's hard to admit it, but I have justified and participated in toxic behavior to avoid being on the receiving end of it. I was a culture killer.

In a past job, the department head was skillfully manipulative. They knew exactly what to say or do to make you feel like you had been punched in the gut or had a puncture wound in your heart. It was painful.

They operated on gossip and fear. I realize now that I lost myself and my values in that position. I gossiped with them and talked badly about people who were frustrating me. And I was rewarded for it. In this messed up way, it felt like I was "good" when I did it.

We're always trying to survive, whether it feels like life or death or is just a matter of avoiding pain. We can find ourselves excusing toxic behaviors in order to protect ourselves. It's never justified, funny, or OK for someone to curse at, berate, belittle, gossip about, or hurt you. *Never.*

But you also play a role in either accepting it, participating in it, or setting a boundary.

I ultimately recognized where I was at fault, set boundaries, and left. I'm stronger and wiser for it now.

Permission to be human. If you know that you need to make these changes too, start by being kind to yourself. You're human. Forgive yourself for not knowing better or doing better. Then make a new choice to step into what is in alignment with your best self—the one that ignites your core values. Going from being a culture killer to a culture keeper starts by being willing to admit and own the parts of you that are out of alignment so that you can grow into the person you truly are, beyond the pain.

When thinking of others, remember that people express themselves on the outside to reflect what they feel on the inside. I've trained myself to not take it personally if someone is spewing negativity—not in order to excuse their behavior but in order to meet them where they are instead of getting triggered into my own anger by their toxic energy. They are clearly suffering; otherwise, they wouldn't act that way. Very few people wake up in the morning and think, "How can I mess up my company's team dynamics and take away trust today? Let me be sure that I take those actions, because the day will be a failure if I don't hurt other people along my path." Most likely they are thinking things like, "Why doesn't anyone understand or support me? How can I ever trust anyone here? No one has my back, and I'm really out on a limb by myself."

In nearly every instance, the "bad guys" think that they're the "good guys" in their stories. I first learned that when I read an article about the mindset of terrorist groups. They present themselves as the saviors, the ones who are leading the way to a better life for their people. It was shocking and illuminating all at once. It made so much sense, especially when we bring it down to our day-to-day interactions. If someone is a culture killer at work, they likely don't see themselves that way.

They are often wounded and feeling unheard, unsupported, or even misunderstood. It's very unlikely that they see themselves as someone who has work to do but instead that everyone else has work to do. The truth is, we all have work to do!

Of course, it's not natural to identify as someone who's the problem. Instead, we identify as the victim of others who are the problem.

When we can lift ourselves out of that mindset and ask for feedback from those who are able to be honest with us, we have a true opportunity to learn, grow, and understand how our behaviors are influencing others.

Permission to be human. If you're in a coaching position, meet that person where they are. Figure out what they're thinking and feeling as your entry point. Because if you go head-in on all the ways they're making things terrible, they won't have the sense that you value psychological safety, vulnerability, or purpose. They deserve a chance at those things too—but only enough chances to show that they're willing to change and do the work. If they don't make that choice, it's time for them to find a new environment where they are a better fit.

Many teams don't have someone on staff who has the skills in coaching and supporting these types of evolutions. You may consider bringing in a relational mediator or an unbiased facilitator to help support conflict resolution between key individuals. Healing for both individuals and teams happens when people don't fear retribution for speaking their truth. This is exactly why I became trained in relational mediation. I knew that it was vital for me to learn how to effectively and confidently guide people toward positive, constructive, healing conversations with one another, instead of around or through someone else. All my workplace mediations since have been successes. People leave feeling relieved, grateful, and hopeful about what's possible in the future. Creating and holding the space for that level of support to happen is worth investing in when you believe in the possibility on the other side of it. On the other hand, if this employee doesn't seem like it's worth that investment and you see no sign of coming together as attainable, it's likely an indication that it's not going to work out.

There's a well-known anecdote that goes like this:

The CFO asks the CEO, "What happens if we invest in developing our people and then they leave us?"

The CEO says, "What happens if we don't and they stay?"

Permission to be human. We all have bad days that we can recover from, so we want to give each other grace and opportunity. Not labeling, but being able to say you know that yesterday was a bad day and that today offers another chance to reset and start again. Culture can be intentionally crafted when you start saying, "We're going to reset; we're going to start again. We have learned, we take responsibility, and will do better now."

Why invest a lot into values and then say, "All right, we're done with that"? This is about integrating and operationalizing, using your values as a way to tune in to ourselves and check in with our team on how we're doing. Because culture can change in an instant, we must constantly be keeping a pulse on how we're doing.

Imagine how different our life experiences would be if we knew how to address and neutralize toxic experiences and behaviors on the spot, if we didn't hold that toxic energy inside us, just waiting to vomit it out on family and friends at the first opportunity. We each play a role in the energy that we create in the world. When you equip your people to respond to and lovingly hold people accountable for the energy they're creating, you have the power to change the world.

When you're intentional about how you craft your culture, you can coach, heal, and eliminate the issues I just described.

Remember, your organization's culture is only as strong as the worst behavior that is allowed, ignored, or gossiped about. When leaders and team members like you create strong guidelines and boundaries around what is in or out of alignment with those values, there is real opportunity to protect your culture from anyone or anything that is putting it at risk. You cannot afford to compromise on your values.

Aligned Culture or Aspirational Culture?

If you have a set of stated values and your behaviors don't reflect them, you do not have an aligned culture. You have an aspirational culture of pie-in-the-sky thinking versus one based in the reality of day-to-day experience.

But when your behaviors are in alignment with those values—boy, you create an incredible place of loyalty, commitment, engagement, pride, and enthusiasm, a place where people are going to stay, regardless of what generation they're a part of. It is something that feels like magic.

Values make us feel alive as individuals and as members of a team. That's what a thriving, intentional culture is about: connecting diverse individuals through a common intrinsic motivator. And values are about as intrinsic as they get. They *naturally* satisfy you. How great is that?

So much of that natural sense of personal satisfaction comes from being able to give of yourself to something that in return gives you pride in being able to make a difference. But there's a fine line that many of us can teeter between, a line that makes a whole world of difference: the divider between passion and stress.

Simon Sinek says, "Working hard for something we don't care about is called stress: Working hard for something we love is called passion."[20] And that sure is the truth! When your work is aligned with your values, passion is ignited. When it's not, stress is sure to come.

I can't tell you how many times I've worked hours on end without even realizing it because I was so excited by the work I was progressing with. I have just as many stories of working on things that took only a few hours but felt like they had taken lifetimes because I didn't care about the work, it wasn't in my passion zone, and it made me feel like I was wasting my energy. When I first started my business and was taking everything on myself, I often had outbursts of anger and regret, including twitchy eyes and sleepless nights that rippled their way into stress for my team.

Your people aren't stressed because they're doing too much— they're stressed because they're doing too little of what aligns with their values. From the experiences that make us come alive to the people who make us cringe, our values define what we stand for in life.

How many of us take the time to discover what they are? And how many of us use them as a guide to direct our environments at work and within ourselves?

When your organization knows, owns, and lives its values, it can be intentional about attracting, retaining, and growing its people through a shared sense of purpose, productivity, and passion. Your results will speak for themselves.

---

20 Simon Sinek (@simonsinek), Twitter, February 28, 2012, 4:20 a.m., https://twitter.com/simonsinek/status/174469085726375936?lang=en.

But when you don't know your values, you will never have a clear compass or guardrails for your culture. This can lead to disengagement, dissatisfaction, and disconnection, both within your team and externally, in terms of your reputation and customers.

As we continue on this journey, you'll become crystal clear on the words that define your team's intrinsic motivators through core values. They'll serve as your compass for success and your guardrails against failure. By recognizing the behaviors that are in or out of alignment with your core values, you'll begin to uncover what's working, things that can be lifted up to create more impact, and what's taking away from your culture and needs to stop or morph accordingly. In that process you'll identify your culture killers and culture keepers, starting by looking in the mirror. What may feel stressful at first will eventually become an act of grace, accountability, and positive energy to fuel your team and organization toward their greatest potential for achievement.

Values Alignment Review

1. Values are intrinsic motivators that represent a person's principles or standards of behavior, one's judgment of what is important in life.

2. Values × Behavior = Culture

3. When you identify the behaviors that are in or out of alignment with your stated core values, you will start to understand what's driving your culture, for better or for worse.

4. Culture keepers are the individuals who lead and maintain the positive aspects of their organization's environment, a reflection of the company's core values. Culture killers are the people who are both actively and passively taking away from a positive work experience.

5. Your people aren't stressed because they're doing too much—they're stressed because they're doing too little of what aligns with their values.

judgment or even punishment kept me from activating my authentic values.

These are the little things that are in fact the massive things, like being confident we're able to show up in life as we are and not be muzzled by others' judgments, bad behavior, or leadership styles. It's my humble opinion that the upcoming generation is shifting this paradigm in a way that is shocking the cultural norms at work—and companies are puzzled by how to respond.

These are not problems that can be solved with a pay increase, a one-time training, or a motivational speech. These things are deeply embedded within us and take dedicated, ongoing support to identify and shift. Few have figured out how to uncover and ignite the connection between our unique set of values and the organic internal drivers that unleash greatness in our everyday work. But I promise you, it is possible. I'm going to teach you how.

Know Your Personal Values

Here's the first step: *Know your personal values.* Get clear on the words that describe your strongest intrinsic motivation—the pieces of your internal compass that drive you and give you a sense of aliveness.

Where do we begin? There are so many options, so I'll give you a couple to choose from.

If you'd like to take an even deeper dive, check out my ten-day audio course on Insight Timer, Know and Live Your Values.

Option 1: Create Your Values Profile

When I'm doing this work with individuals and companies, they use my online Values Inventory Survey to generate what I call a values profile. What's cool about it is that it's 100 percent based on what the individual selected, not some kind of algorithm that determines what color, number, or personality type you are (any fellow ENFJs in the house?). Although those are all helpful tools, my system of self-reflection on and organization of your personal values can give you more leeway to get curious and explore the nooks and crannies of your uniqueness. But not everyone is into that type of broad processing, and that's OK too.

The following is a free-form Values Inventory Survey that will work perfectly if you want to do it right now.

Before you begin to look at these values, set your intention. You can do that by asking yourself, "Why do I want to know my values? What feeling do I want to have as a result of this work?"

Once you have a clear answer, take three long, deep breaths, close your eyes, and repeat in your mind or out loud, "I will be open, honest, and loving to myself as I identify my authentic values."

Hold your intention throughout this exercise and the rest of your time doing this work.

Across the top of the page of a blank sheet of paper, write out the following headers in a line: "This Drives Me," "I *Wish* This Drove Me," "This Describes Me," and "This Does *Not* Resonate."

"This Drives Me" indicates something that really motivates you. You could even say it's unshakably who you are.

"I *Wish* This Drove Me" is more about being honest with yourself. You aspire to be this way, but it's not your current experience. And that is OK.

"This Describes Me" indicates something that is a part of what's important to you but doesn't necessarily motivate you.

And finally, "This Does *Not* Resonate" is the most self-explanatory. It indicates something that simply doesn't resonate with you. It's neither good nor bad. It just is.

These will be the categories that you will be using to classify each value for yourself.

What's very important during this exercise is that you are honest with yourself. For example, if I am honest with myself, when I hear the value of health, I have to put it in the "I *Wish* This Drove Me" category because I think it's very important, but I'm not currently someone who is motivated to exercise regularly—although I wish I were. That's not to say that I couldn't be in the future; I simply am not actively exercising at this present time in my life.

Notice that I describe health as related to exercise. You might have a totally different definition. And that's OK.

I'm intentionally *not* providing definitions for each of the words I'm about to share because we all interpret words differently. Only focus on what that word means to *you*, just like I did with the example of health. You don't need to google it or ask someone else their opinion; simply tap into your own intuition, and trust that whatever you believe it means is correct. Because when it comes to your values, that is so very true.

When you are selecting a category, try not to spend too much time debating where it should fall. If you're torn, revisit it later; you can always change it in the future.

There is no right or wrong way to do this. As long as you're being honest with yourself, you are doing this from a good place.

The following list of words represents some of the most common values across gender, ethnicity, age, and socioeconomic class. They primarily come from the research behind the Schwartz

Values Scale.[21] However, it is important to note that this is not a complete list, so please know that there will be time to add any that are missing for you.

As you read each of these words, place them under one of your columns. Ask yourself, "Does this drive me? Do I wish it drove me? Does it describe me? Not resonate with me?" These are the categories you captured before.

Let's begin. The first one is adventure.

Does adventure drive you? Is it something you wish drove you? Does it describe you? Or does adventure not resonate with you?

Without judgment, write the word *adventure* under whichever column makes the most sense to you.

Let's keep going. Again, don't take too much time deliberating on these. Simply go with what comes to mind; you can always adjust later.

Do the same gut check with each of the following words:

adventure	excellence	imagination
ambition	exciting life	independence
authenticity	family security	influence
cleanliness	freedom	inner harmony
community	generosity	innovation
connection	gratitude	integrity
creativity	growth	intelligence
curiosity	health	kindness
daring	helpfulness	knowledge
empathy	honesty	learning
empowerment	humility	loyalty
equality	humor	mature love

---

21   Shalom H. Schwartz, "An Overview of the Schwartz Theory of Basic Values," *Online Readings in Psychology and Culture* 2, no. 1 (December 2012), https://doi.org/10.9707/2307-0919.1116.

openness	religion	stability
organization	respect for tradition	success
pleasure	responsibility	true friendship
politeness	self-care	trust
public image	self-discipline	unity with nature
purpose	self-respect	varied life
racial justice	sense of belonging	vulnerability
reciprocation	social justice	wealth
reflection	spiritual life	wisdom

Now that you can see your lists, let's take some time to look over the categories.

Everything listed in the "This Drives Me" column represents your core values—the aspects of yourself that motivate and drive you toward or away from different things.

Everything listed in the "I *Wish* This Drove Me" column is an aspirational value. These describe what you aspire to become.

The ones that describe you are values you hold, but they are not drivers. For example, I hold the value of politeness, but I don't wake up in the morning excited or driven to be polite. But you might. And whether you do or you don't, it's beautiful to know that about yourself.

Finally, the ones that don't resonate are exactly what they sound like: they simply aren't things that resonate with you personally—and remember, that's OK.

Option 2: Track Your Values in Real Time

Often we don't know the words for our values, like *independence, health, inner harmony, curiosity, freedom,* or whatever else. And that's likely because you've never thought about whether you behave in alignment with your values in real time. For example, I love collaborating with open-minded professionals because it gives me a sense of belonging (one of my core values). However, I really dislike collaborating with professionals who object to trying creative new approaches because it generates a lack of belonging. So I feel a sense of belonging when collaboration is enjoyable. I do not feel a sense of belonging when collaboration is not enjoyable. Both scenarios are prime examples of experiences we might easily write off as "really liking my team" versus "working with a bunch of jerks." When you dig a little deeper beneath the visceral response, there is a core value in there that's either being activated or shut down inside of you. Make sense?

If you really want to go on this journey, one of the best things to do is to start taking note of those moments. When coaching people one-on-one, I'll give them a one-week assignment: Set the intention to go on a nonjudgmental, conscious journey toward knowing your values. Then every day of that week, write down the experiences that make you feel the most alive and the ones that make you feel the most drained. Make note of whom you're with, what's going on, and what you notice. It's helpful to have a pocket notepad or mobile note app handy to keep them all in one place. You may choose to do this in real time or perhaps opt for a regular download at the end of the day. Simply ask yourself to identify where your energy was high and low and make a note of it.

I feel most alive when I'm in nature. A specific example appropriate for this exercise is as follows:

- Writing under "my tree" at Fort McHenry. Enjoying the ground under my bare feet, the wind rustling through the tree, the ability to feel alone and productive while still in a public place.

Just bullet it out; it can be at a high level but should have enough detail that it serves as a mnemonic device.

Here's an example of the opposite:

- Going to a networking event. Feeling obligated to make trivial conversation with people who want to pitch me their services. Being drained by how much of it seems to be about getting photos for social media instead of building meaningful relationships. Wishing I were at home with my family instead of building my network.

Now let's pretend that you've collected all those emotional data points from your day and look at them through a values lens. We can reverse engineer your values from here by uncovering what lies beneath the surface of the experience.

If it's an experience that lights you up and brings you energy, it's something that reflects your values. In my first example about writing under my tree, the values that live in that experience (for me) are unity with nature, connection, and inner harmony. (If you need ideas for words to pull from, look at the values list shown earlier in option 1.)

If it's an experience that's draining you, it's likely one of two things: It's draining because it's missing your value, or it reflects a value that doesn't resonate with you. In my example of networking events, I'm missing the values of sense of belonging, connection, and family stability. The value of public image does not resonate with me. Thank goodness, though, that there are people who do get jazzed about these types of events.

Write down the value(s) that are connected to each experience and then tally them up. See which come up the most often and which are less apparent. From there, you can identify what motivates you the most often and what might be available for you to tap into more. Now categorize your values like we did in the first option: This Drives Me (core value), I Wish This Drove Me (aspirational value), This Describes Me (value), and This Does Not Resonate (not a value).

Permission to be human. The world isn't designed for all my wants and needs to be met at every cocktail reception. Where would we be today without people who get lit up by the work that drains us? Relatedly, if a value doesn't resonate with you, that's not to say it's a bad value. That's what makes us all unique, different, and wonderful, and we get to live in this dynamic universe together because we have different values. This internal energy feedback can help you to understand where you most authentically belong so that you don't have to chameleon your way into a place where you're not truly being you. It's much easier to go on a journey to find your people than force yourself to be someone you're not. Not everyone or every place is going to click for you—and that's OK. It's what makes you human.

Double-Checking Your Values List

Whether you chose option 1 to create a values profile to categorize your values by name or option 2 to reverse engineer your values by tracking your life experiences, let's reflect further.

Looking over your values categories, what do you notice? Does this feel like an accurate picture of you? What trends are clear? What might be missing? If a core value is missing for you personally, this is a great time to add it in.

For example, if sisterhood or brotherhood is something that drives you and it's not on this list, simply add it. Do that with any words that represent values that matter to you, and don't worry about doing it perfectly. You'll know what matters as you continue in your values discovery process.

Some Values Are Constant; Others Change

Fairly often I'm asked about whether your values stick with you for life. It's a great question. As with all this work, it's a case-by-case answer. Overall, our core values tend to stay pretty constant. Meaning the things that drive us often do for most of our lives. However, life experiences (in particular, milestone moments—those times when you felt incredibly high and when you felt painfully low) can dramatically change us and therefore change our values.

My husband and I create a new value profile every year to take inventory of what's stayed the same and what's changed. When we first started, spiritual life did not resonate with either of us. We thought it was some mumbo-jumbo stuff that people told themselves to feel better. But after a life-changing shamanic retreat, we transformed that thinking. Spirituality now drives us more than anything! We have monthly manifestation ceremonies, set daily intentions, have deep gratitude for our spirit guides, and lean on the wisdom of our ancestors regularly. If my younger self saw me now, she'd be very confused even by the sentence I just wrote. And today I've never been clearer.

This type of shift was also transparent for a dear friend, colleague, and participant in our values alignment work. Nikki James Zellner had a solid grasp of her values after working together regularly, and she could identify and articulate them with confidence. When she began her values journey nearly five years prior, advocacy did not resonate with her. It's not that she had an issue with it; it just wasn't something on her radar that lit her up or motivated her to action. Then one afternoon she received an unexpected and urgent call from her sons' day care. They had been poisoned by carbon monoxide. Naturally, Nikki was devastated. Her sons were not well, and they could have died if they weren't removed from the building when they were.

In an instant milestone moment, she channeled her fear into positive action. After doing initial research, she learned that it was not required for day cares to have carbon monoxide detectors. Outraged by this blatant oversight in the health and well-being of children all over the state, she painstakingly started to become an advocate. Reaching out to her local government, she ultimately made her way through the ranks to pass legislation that now requires all day cares to have carbon monoxide detectors. It was a huge undertaking that had its highs and lows, but through it all, she was energized by and proud of her new core value of advocacy.

Just like Nikki and me, you likely have these moments too. Perhaps a time where you walked into an experience as one person and left it as someone else. Health issues, loss of loved ones, and receiving miracles are often triggers for such change. When we have the wherewithal to vocalize our values, we can see what shifts and what remains the same through the ups and downs of life. So keep checking back in with yourself to more fully embrace the truest you today.

Cultivating Your Values

As you take the wisdom you gained from this exercise, set an intention to keep that awareness alive beyond this moment. When you're feeling in or out of alignment with these parts of yourself, connect a value or a few values to what is either being activated or, alternatively, feels like it's missing. Notice which values come up the most around your extreme highs and lows. They are signs of what your truest core values are. Intentional value reflection can be ignited by keeping a journal; talking to a loved one about it; or creating a daily, weekly, or monthly check-in about the alignment of your actions with your values. The more you can be mindful about how you're living and where adjustment can be made, the more likely you are to feel a sense of personal mastery and self-love for giving yourself permission to be fully human.

In my own life, I found that I had the intention to embody the value of health. Health was very much an aspirational value in my life. That's because when it came to my daily choices, I wasn't truly in alignment with my definition of health. So I turned to my partner, who just so happens to be a health coach (go figure!) and asked him for support with creating an ongoing movement and stretching routine as well as help with being more mindful of my nutrition. With him as my witness, inspiration, and coach, I was able to slowly but surely make the shifts. One step at a time, without judgment of pace. It was also key that I was kind and generous with myself because it's not easy to change. I would never truly adopt a new lifestyle if I were beating myself up in my mind about my progress all day.

Consider these reflection prompts as you cultivate your values further:

- What are my top three core values in this season of life?

- How do I personally define them?

- Who or what experiences instilled this value in me?

- How has this value shown up in my life?

- Where might I be able to activate this value more intentionally?

- Where might I celebrate this value in action?

- Who in my life could support my embodiment of this value?

Values-Driven Communities

Needing loving accountability and support is precisely why we developed values-driven communities. We wanted to create a space where people who cared about living in alignment with their values could come together and be supported.

> Both through our Journey to Alignment six-week cohort program and our Community of Alignment monthly group coaching, we've had so many curious souls trust that values were a way to reach their greatest levels of happiness, peace, and power.

As a result, they have completely transformed into values-aligned experts in their own lives. Taking ownership of their choices each day, falling down and getting back up, and reclaiming their power to activate their values in the face of society wanting otherwise for them. The ripple effects have also been significant. Their partners, children, and colleagues have all been impacted by their inner work, and many of them are now teaching others the way to know, own, and live their values. It was so powerful that it inspired us to create an apprenticeship around this work. The more of us who live this way, the better our world will become.

You don't need expert support to have accountability and connection to your values in community. You can simply go on a mission to find your tribe that ignites your vibe. Unity with nature lights you up? How about finding a hiking club? Innovation gets you stoked? How about attending a conference on the latest technologies? Family stability makes you feel the most grounded? How about investing in a membership to a local museum that you know you'll visit with your family regularly? In the end, it doesn't have to be all that complicated. If you leave the experience filled with energy, then you know you're on the right track to activating your values with intention.

Permission to be human. Whatever you do, be generous, kind, and gracious about your personal evolution and journey. You're amazing just as you are now.

Values Work Is Deep Work

Whenever I facilitate this work with organizations, it's a two- to three-day retreat experience, where the first full day is all about the individual. We start by walking each person through the process of naming their values and then connecting them to their life experiences. We're not just born with this set of values; they are typically instilled in us by others—for better or for worse. When we take the time to honor our past, we can make sense of our values in a much more meaningful way than just picking words off a list.

For example, in my Know and Live Your Values audio course, Life Lens retreat, or multiday Values Retreats, making this list is the easiest part.

We then do a deep dive into looking at your milestone moments, and we map them out in terms of your entire life. Then, using our values profile, we overlay our values onto each milestone moment, seeing apparent trends and clear frontrunners for the values that matter most to you as an individual.

This process could easily be a full week, month, year, or lifetime thing, should you have the interest and commitment to the work.

When you do this type of reflection, a lot of the work doesn't feel good in the moment. It's challenging, it's difficult, it's uncomfortable. In a recent corporate values retreat, one of the participants noted that he'd never looked this deeply into himself and it was making him upset. He didn't understand what this personal work had to do with the company's values and why he wasn't able to do this work with ease. I was so impressed that he had the energy to speak up and articulate what was going on in his internal dialogue. It helped every other person in the room who was experiencing any level of that feeling too. It also gave me an awesome framework from which to explain why it mattered so much for each person to go within before looking outward. One thing always rings true: You cannot sustainably embrace or operationalize your values if you don't have self-awareness. It's necessary for everyone to know that self-awareness is a long game that's typically not easy, fast, and fun.

In an article in *Fast Company* magazine, Mary Slaughter and David Rock of the NeuroLeadership Institute wrote,

> Unfortunately, the trend in many organizations is to design learning to be as easy as possible. Aiming to respect their employees' busy lives, companies build training programs that can be done at any time, with no prerequisites, and often on a mobile

device. The result is fun and easy training programs that employees rave about (making them easier for developers to sell) but [that] don't actually instill lasting learning.

Worse still, programs like these may lead employers to optimize for misleading metrics, like maximizing for "likes" or "shares" or high "net promoter scores," which are easy to earn when programs are fun and fluent but not when they're demanding. Instead of designing for recall or behavior change, we risk designing for popularity.[22]

Reflecting on the same issue, Brené Brown has stated, "The reality is that to be effective, learning needs to be effortful. That's not to say that anything that makes learning easier is counterproductive—or that all unpleasant learning is effective. The key here is desirable difficulty. The same way you feel a muscle 'burn' when it's being strengthened, the brain needs to feel some discomfort when it's learning. Your mind might hurt for a while—but that's a good thing."[23]

How Your Values Connect to Your Company's Values

There's often pushback from employees who don't understand why they have to focus so much on themselves; they say, "Isn't this about the company?" When that happens, it gives me the incredible opportunity to educate and empower them in understanding

22 Mary Slaughter and David Rock, "No Pain, No Brain Gain: Why Learning Demands (a Little) Discomfort)," *Fast Company*, April 30, 2018, https://www.fastcompany.com/40560075/ no-pain-no-brain-gain-why-learning-demands-a-little-discomfort.

23 Brown, 170.

that culture is created by the behaviors of every single one of us. Our behaviors are a reflection of our values. When we take the time to honor our values and understand where they were born and enhanced, we start the process of not only knowing but also owning our values. Values are far from a matter of superficial box-checking, but again, they often are presented that way.

We could just jump straight into the values of the company, and that would likely be more comfortable for most organizations. However, comfort is not what makes us grow and gain greater, more profound wisdom about ourselves and our community. When we skip the personal knowing, we pass over the opportunity to understand how unique yet similar we all are on a human level. We skip the realization that by knowing ourselves better, we understand our culture better and can be better advocates for the values that motivate us individually and collectively.

Values work is deep work. If we were doing surface-level work, we wouldn't be doing the work that was required to make meaningful shifts within the culture. Although consultants can illuminate, measure, guide, advise, coach, and support the change, you and your people must take responsibility and ownership of the culture—and the only way that culture can change is when people have self-awareness and accountability.

When you understand what your personal values are and where they came from, you can better understand how you are showing up in or out of alignment with the company's core values. From that place, you can then empower yourself and ask others to hold you accountable to these core values, knowing what kind of environment you want to create with others.

Culture work is some of the hardest work because it's the people work. It's the emotion work. It's the self-awareness work. Each one of us is such a complicated and unique human being.

When we take the time to know who we ourselves are, it gives us the opportunity to know other people.

Often we look to others to do the work; we think culture is someone else's responsibility. It's the CEO's job, it's HR's job, it's the leadership's job. Even if you have a chief culture officer, I'm here to tell you that it's still the job of each and every person within that company to intentionally gain self-awareness and feedback to see what work exists for them in terms of how they're creating the culture every day. The leadership can surely set the tone, provide the coaching, and ensure that guidance is available, but an aligned culture exists only when everyone understands and owns their role in crafting it each day.

Whether you feel like you're in complete alignment with your values or you have no idea what they are, this work will serve you in knowing how you—and therefore your organization—can step up in more authentically living your core values. Self-awareness of our intrinsic motivators, sparked by activation of our values, enables us to name and get curious about the experiences, behaviors, and conditions that are required for a sense of personal alignment, purpose, and productivity each day.

Although this work might be uncomfortable at first, remember that you are a conscious leader who's choosing to dig in and gain wisdom from the discomfort.

> And if you want support, we have lots of it to offer you.

When you take responsibility for your values being activated, you can teach others how to do the same.

Values Alignment Review

1. To know your personal values, get clear on the words that describe your strongest intrinsic motivation—the pieces of your internal compass that drive you and give you a sense of aliveness.

2. Core values drive you. Values describe you. Aspirational values are those you wish drove you. And some don't resonate with you at all, not ever making it as one of your values.

3. We're not born with a set of values; they are typically instilled in us by others—for better or for worse. When we take the time to honor our past, we can make sense of our values in a much more meaningful way than just picking words off a list.

4. You cannot sustainably embrace or operationalize your values if you don't have self-awareness.

5. Values work is deep work. If we were doing surface-level work, we wouldn't be doing the work that was required to make meaningful shifts within the culture.

This chapter highlighted:
- Our ten-day Know and Live Your Values audio course on Insight Timer
- The Journey to Alignment six-week values alignment cohort program
- Values Retreats for individuals and teams
- Community of Alignment ongoing values integration support

If any of these opportunities sparked your interest, learn more at www.permissiontobehuman.co, or check out the SparkVision Resources section of this book.

This is why we offer Values Retreats and online training programs; we even have an apprenticeship for people who have a calling to embody this work.

When you can expertly navigate these conversations, astonishing energy, connections, and power are ignited. Inevitably, through this work, we always learn that we are so much more alike than not, even if that wasn't clear before.

I've had retreat participants say, "We came in today as colleagues and left as family." Or even, "I never got along with that team member before, and now I get that we butt heads because we're so alike. We're both planning to get coffee together now to build our relationship and talk more about our shared values."

Pretty powerful stuff, right? Now it's time for you to ignite that type of power within your team.

Uncovering Your Values

Step 1: Narrow down the list of words that will ultimately become your core values.

Drawing from the design of the Values Inventory Survey in chapter 4, gather a list of your team's personal core values. Remember, this is so that we build off what already intrinsically motivates your people individually and collectively. Using the list from chapter 4 (adding your own values that apply), create a simple survey for team members to select up to five personal core values. Include an open text box if team members have a core value that's not listed that they'd like to add. Do your best to get 100 percent participation, and do not move forward unless the majority of team members weigh in.

Step 2: Tally and total the outcomes. See which core values are the most frequently named and narrow your list down to the top ten. If there are ties, expand or contract this list accordingly. You will get a truly dynamic picture of where most people overlap and where there are some outliers (remember, this is neither good nor bad; it just is).

Step 3: Share the top results with everyone and ask for feedback. Trust me—people find this to be fascinating, and it ignites healthy curiosity and conversation. When you share the list, ask people to look at it now through the lens of your organization. Ask, "Do any additional values need to be added to the list that are key to how you accomplish your work today? What makes us stand out from other companies, and how does this motivate team members toward our mission and vision?" You may then learn that your list is good as is. Or you may learn that you need to add a few additional core values. If there are more, add them to the potential core values list. Do not feel the need to edit it down quite yet. This is the time to encourage participation and creative thinking. No one is wrong in what they share. Again, it is not about getting it perfect; it is about having voices heard and creating buy-in.

Step 4: Connect through values storytelling. With the updated values list complete and shared, ask your team members to reflect on this question: "What was a significant time that you experienced at least one of these values in action here at work?" Put your people in small groups to have these conversations. It's a bonus if you can intentionally place them in groups that are a mix of different departments. After giving them ample time to share their stories, encourage each group to select one to present to the organization at large. When this occurs, others outside of their intimate conversation benefit from the additional positive energy around the values that are already ignited within your company's culture.

Permission to be human. This process of reflection and connection is necessary for people to tap into their emotional intelligence and understand how values are already embodied at work and why they matter so much. This exercise puts folks into the mindset of what's possible instead of getting stuck in what isn't. It reminds them that they already know the language of values, and it's just a prompt of how to curate and focus on what ignites alignment for them as a member of your team.

Step 5: Invite each team member to cast three votes toward the values they believe are the best fit for both the company and their personal intrinsic motivators. A survey works perfectly here.

Permission to be human. Be clear on the power of each team member's vote. Encourage them to vote on the values that they're willing and expecting to be held accountable for—not platitudes but the true north. Make sure they know their votes are saying, "I'm willing to look in the mirror to see what I need to do for my behavior to reflect this value. Hold me accountable. This is the culture and community I want and choose to be a part of. Hold me accountable. I know that means I have the opportunity to learn and grow. Hold me accountable. I will do my best to show up this way, but I know that we're all learning. Hold me accountable so that I can better understand the opportunities that exist in my development and leadership."

It's important that they have this framework to understand what exactly they're voting on and that it's more than just the updated language on your website.

Step 6: Finalize your values. Once you get your votes back, it should be clear which (up to six) core values ring true for the majority of your team. And know that it's not going to be 100 percent across the board. The idea is to own the ones that are clear trends and unifiers. If the trends aren't clear, do a second vote using just the top winners.

This may feel excessive to some, but it's well worth the extra investment to ensure that people feel it's a fair process. You don't want to lose trust at this stage. So know that this is an effective and engaging way to guide your company toward its purpose.

Defining Your Values

Step 7: Create your unique core value definitions. Once you have your core values confirmed through a democratic process, it is time to define them. Not by what a dictionary says but in terms of what they mean to your company—because I bet that my personal definition of a certain value is different from yours. Think about it. Let's choose authenticity. If my company has the value of authenticity, I might personally define it as "showing up completely as I am." But your company might define it as "being true to our mission, vision, and values at all times." Both of these are great—and they're very different. Don't assume that you're all speaking the same values language. Define your values clearly so that you're all on the same page.

Here are some pointers on how to do this:

- Narrow the values definitions down to one to two succinct sentences. This is a best practice so that your people can easily recall what the value stands for and how it applies to them as individuals and as a unit.

- Make sure that your definition is specifically for your organization, not a generalized concept for all.

- Ensure that it applies to your internal culture *and* in the way you present yourself out in the world, in your community, with your customers and clients.

- Don't use the value word itself within the definition.

- Be mindful that the definitions are distinct to each value instead of overlapping content or concepts throughout.

- Begin with a verb to show the action that you're taking as it relates to that value.

To create these definitions, empower small groups of team members to take the first go. Allow them to think through and pull together words that feel like an accurate definition of how your company will take ownership of each value. This exercise will provide the first round of idea generation. It will be a springboard for your communication team to work their magic. Once all the small groups have their definitions ready, pull them together and have your branding experts finesse the final language so that the words flow together and are a cohesive presentation of what you stand for. Make the tweaks needed while honoring the work and sentiments of the small groups.

Step 8: Confirm your values definitions. Once you feel that you have a cohesive set of values, send them out for another round of feedback. Again, this is about trust and buy-in. There's no room to break trust by skipping this step.

I recommend that you engage this feedback through a Values Connection Survey. With a basic yes or no response, ask people:

- Can we commit to this?

- Does this reflect what we stand for?

- Does this motivate and inspire you?

Include an open text box for any additional feedback. Once you have the results in, revisit any of the definitions that don't have majority agreement among team members. If you don't have majority agreement, go back to the drawing board with the team that created the original definition, review the feedback, and see what appropriate changes can be made. Then do a final round of voting using the same questions as before but offering only the value(s) that need to be reworked.

Permission to be human. Typically, at this stage you're golden. And if you're not, that's OK too. Be kind, gentle, and considerate of where you choose to move forward and where you choose to dig deeper. Remember, it is not about getting 100 percent agreement; it's about getting the vast majority of team members to be in agreement. If you have 100 percent agreement on everything, you likely have a small team or don't work with humans. We're more complex than that.

During the pandemic, SparkVision went to a live online format to facilitate a three-day values retreat with The Pittsburgh Foundation team. They are an incredibly thoughtful, articulate, and passionate group who deeply cares about cementing their core values into the foundation of their culture. Our experience together was simply profound.

And our process went exactly as it was outlined here. After the live retreat, small value groups convened on their own to finalize their core value definitions (step 7). A survey was then sent for feedback from the whole team (step 8). Based on the results, we regrouped with one of the values subgroups and the foundation's communication team to do the second round of edits. That led us to a final survey to get the staff's response to the updated definitions, and there was powerful feedback.

Each step was key to ensuring that we truly made it clear as to what was expected for their team to own their company's values. Here's what we ignited and what we adopted as their core values:

Accountability: We act with transparency and integrity, fulfilling our commitments and owning the outcomes of our decisions.

Collaboration: We unite in our work together to increase its impact in our community for the collective greater good.

Community: We embrace the opportunity to learn from those we serve and those who serve us to help shape the spaces that bring us together.

Racial Justice: We work to enact fundamental systemic changes by eliminating policies, laws, practices, attitudes and cultural messages that reinforce differential outcomes by race.

Trust: We have faith in our communities and earn their confidence by demonstrating competency, honesty and positive intent.

Pretty powerful statements here, right?

Step 9: Honor and celebrate your work. Once your core values are finalized, it's time to share them with others and celebrate. As in truly celebrate the effort, intention, and energy that was invested in knowing and owning your company's values. More on this in chapter 7. It's a big deal and deserves an announcement (both internally and externally) with a tone of positive energy about its meaning. Perhaps you want to send a special announcement out to your LISTSERV, create thoughtfully designed marketing collateral, send a press release, or maybe even make a video about the experience of uncovering your values. You never know what you might inspire in others too!

Starting Point 2: Further Develop Current Values

What if you fall into the category of having values but not really knowing them or using them beyond your marketing collateral? Or perhaps different departments have come up with their own values and they've never been unified across the organization. The latter is more common than I realized and has the potential to create a significant fracture in your culture.

Think about it: How can you truly have a cohesive culture if some people are operating based on one set of values and another is operating with completely different ones? I've worked with many hospitals and universities, and this was commonplace for them. Essentially, the institutions had gone through a strategic effort to create one set of shared core values, but other departments either didn't know about them or didn't have accountability to them because they decided that they needed to create their own. I get that an IT department could have different intrinsic motivators from a sales department, but that doesn't mean they should be exempt from the overarching intention of how that organization accomplishes their work. In those instances, it would be meaningful to use the overarching values for discussion in how they can truly own them within their team. With a little bit of thoughtful reflection, new possibilities are born from the same solid foundation.

Permission to be human. If you plan to make this type of change, be sure to reach out to the specific teams that have their own sets of values so that they understand why and how this process will take place. Thank them for their dedication to their values and ask them to join you in creating a unified approach together. You don't want to assume that others are on board because you said so. You want to ignite in them an excitement that comes from being a part of the positive shift together.

Step 1: Determine whether you're keeping or reevaluating your core values. First, take a good, hard look at them and decide whether you want to forge ahead with what you've got or whether it's time for a refresh.

You can start that with the Values Alignment Survey. Ask your people (and once again, I mean all of them) whether these are accurate values for your company. Use a 10-point scale (0 = not at all, 5 = somewhat, 10 = completely) for the following questions for each of your core values (replacing X for your core values and Y for their definitions):

1. X value is defined as Y. Do you believe that this is an accurate description of this value for our company's culture? (1–10 scale)

2. What is your perception of how effectively X is lived across the organization? (1–10 scale)

3. What is your perception of how effectively X is lived across your team? (1–10 scale)

4. What is your perception of how effectively *you* live X? (1–10 scale)

5. *Bonus question*: What company experiences and/or staff member(s) positively represent the value of X? (Follow with an open text box.)

The bonus question can be used in many ways, but at the very least, it is an opportunity for you to recognize your culture keepers and your proven practices when it comes to leading in alignment with your values. I talk much more about this in chapter 9.

Step 2: Share the data. If you don't plan to use this data, then don't ask for it. It can make people feel like they wasted their energy if you don't present and use it for positive change that they took the time to submit.

Whenever I am building culture keeper programs within companies, I use the bonus question to determine who is already embodying the values by creating daily proven practices. No matter their tenure, title, or rank, they are seen as the experts for guiding cultural alignment and help to ignite positive shifts through strategic, ongoing efforts to bring the values to life within the entire organization. When it comes to sharing that list, tune in to your intuition to determine whether that would ignite a popularity contest sort of vibe or if it would make sense to let those people know in a more strategic way.

It's always fascinating to see the difference between how people view themselves and how they view their teams and the company at large. Nine out of ten times, the individual believes that their personal behavior is more aligned with the company's stated core values than with their teams or their organization. It leaves me wondering who is creating this disconnected culture in which each individual seems to feel that they're doing a great job but no one around them is. *Funny how we humans are, isn't it?*

Step 3: Determine next steps. This data will give you a dynamic starting point to have a deeper conversation about and understanding of how to best move forward from a place that serves the individual and the company. You may choose to start afresh, or you might just change the definitions. You'll have better direction once you've reviewed the feedback from your team. If you decide to start over, follow the steps listed in starting point 1.

Owning Your Values Requires Constant Maintenance

Values ownership is not something that locks into place and stays there without maintenance. Think of it this way: Let's say that you have a top-of-the-line car with all the bells and whistles that runs so smoothly that you feel like you're one with the road every time you turn the key in the ignition. Over time, the interior accumulates dust, dirt from your shoes, and the extra stuff that you throw in the back seat. And it not only needs to be charged up but also tuned up every five thousand miles. You have choices. You can do the ongoing maintenance to ensure that it stays clean and running smoothly. Or you can allow it all to pile up and then have to make a hefty investment to get the stains out of the carpet and replace parts of the engine that were ignored. What's the point of investing in this fancy mode of transportation if it is only going to have temporary results?

The same goes for your company's values. They're a practice that requires constant maintenance. There's endless opportunity for reflection, change, and growth.

This values work is designed so that every single person at your company has the opportunity to know themselves better through their shared core values. You can see that it's not a superficial exercise that we're going through. You must know yourself before you can really know anyone else. We must all come together and have these meaningful conversations about what matters to all of us before we can be intentional about the culture that we want to create every single day.

So I thank you for sitting through the discomfort, for seeing it as an opportunity for greater self-awareness to arise. When you solidify your shared core values in this communal way, it sends the message that your entire team cares about them. You're all saying, "This is what we're united through. This is how we accomplish our work. This is how I stand up as an individual in this organization, and it gives me a sense of purpose and meaning when I do that."

That's where we're headed.

Whether you're creating values from scratch or adjusting your current values, you now have the steps required to take action. And by taking those steps, grounded in reflection, connection, and growth, you are igniting those very feelings within each of your team members. When you genuinely know where you are (instead of assuming and starting from where you want to be), you can use it as a gauge for where you and your company *can* go. When your values and your work are in alignment, every single day is filled with purpose, no matter what you're doing. It's a beautiful experience that we all deserve to have in life. You have the power to ignite that for your team.

Alignment with your company's core values is within you and each of your team members—you just need to choose to behave with those values, and not against them, to activate that alignment.

Values Alignment Review

1. Values are not created; they're uncovered.

2. Your company is in one of two places right now: (1) you don't have defined values yet or (2) you have defined values but you want to develop and integrate them further. No matter where you fall, you're exactly where you're meant to be.

3. Involve your entire company in the process of identifying your values. Engage your people to weigh in on what's real—not just what's aspirational or contains the buzzwords for your industry at that time.

4. Every single day, every single action is ultimately a reflection or disconnection of your values.

5. Your culture has the chance to thrive when your values serve as your compass and guardrails for success. When you solidify your shared core values in this communal way, it sends the message that your entire team cares about them.

This chapter highlighted our:
- Values Alignment Guide Apprenticeship program
- Permission to Be Human online training program
- Values Retreats for individuals and teams

If any of these opportunities sparked your interest, learn more at www.permissiontobehuman.co, or check out the SparkVision Resources section of this book.

Section II: Own and Live Your Values

CHAPTER 6

Value Promises™

Integrity is choosing courage over comfort; choosing what is right over what is fun, fast, or easy; and choosing to practice our values rather than simply professing them.
—Brené Brown

E very organization's wins and losses are tied to the behaviors of the individuals who work there. When your team's behaviors (and especially those of the leaders) emulate your company's core values, others will follow. It's as if you opened the door for them to walk through with you.

Values are just nice ideas until your day-to-day exchanges are aligned with what you publicly declare. When that happens, authenticity is the result. And when they do not, distrust and toxicity spread.

Take the famous case of Enron as a prime example of an organization that proclaimed certain values but behaved in contradiction to them.

Enron was founded in 1985, and its annual revenues were over $100 billion by 2000. *Fortune* magazine named them America's Most Innovative Firm for six consecutive years. Their core values included communication, integrity, respect, and excellence. Yet at the end of 2001, it was revealed that Enron's reported financial condition was sustained by an institutionalized, systemic, and creatively planned accounting fraud. Enron has become a well-known example of willful corporate fraud and corruption. What happened to communication, integrity, respect, and excellence?

Although this is clearly an extreme case, many of our own companies are off when it comes to the disconnect between our behaviors and our stated values. How can you pinpoint the behaviors you expect of others without making assumptions? How do you know how to hold yourself and others lovingly accountable when those expectations aren't met? Over this next chapter, you'll learn exactly how to answer those questions so that you and your team have a transparent guide for aligning your behaviors and choices with your company's core values.

Own Your Values

Now that you know how your values—for yourself and for your company—are defined, it's time to own them with even more conviction. And I mean own them like you'd own your top revenue-generating product or process. Without ownership, they have no weight. With ownership, your values are life giving.

Employee engagement is correlated to the extent to which employees feel passionate about their jobs, are committed to the organization, and put discretionary effort into their work.[24] Therefore, owning your values is one of the most significant ways you can increase your employee engagement. What better way to ignite intrinsic motivation? Core values (when in alignment

---

24 Custom Insight, "What Is Employee Engagement?" accessed April 28, 2021, https://www.custominsight.com/employee-engagement-survey/what-is-employee-engagement.asp.

with individuals' beliefs) empower your people to do the right thing without asking for permission or questioning themselves. Deciding that they matter and making that evident in your actions will transform everyone's day-to-day.

Research shows us the following:

- Companies with engaged workers grew revenue two and a half times more than companies with less engaged workers (Bain & Company).[25]

- Organizations with high employee engagement outperform those with low employee engagement by 202 percent (Gallup).[26]

- Highly engaged workplaces see a 10 percent increase in customer ratings and a 20 percent increase in sales (Gallup).[27]

Remember, it's not about coming up with abstract, aspirational commitments to your values that you'll then impose on your company. It's about identifying what matters most to your company through behaviors like how your teams talk and act, how learning and growth are fostered, and what criteria you use to define success and failure. This is a chance for you and your

25 Domenico Azzarello, Frédéric Debruyne, and Ludovica Mottura, "The Chemistry of Enthusiasm," Bain & Company, May 4, 2012, https://www.bain.com/insights/the-chemistry-of-enthusiasm.

26 Gallup, "Engage Your Employees to See High Performance and Innovation," accessed November 14, 2020, https://www.gallup.com/workplace/229424/employee-engagement.aspx.

27 Jim Harter and Annamarie Mann, "The Right Culture: Not Just about Employee Satisfaction," Gallup, April 12, 2017, https://www.gallup.com/workplace/236366/right-culture-not-employee-satisfaction.aspx.

team to make promises that you're willing and expecting to be held accountable to.

Expectations – Agreement = Disappointment

Expectations – Agreement = Disappointment is one of my favorite formulas because it makes so much sense. I was given this gem by my community colleague, leadership coach, and cherished friend Lori Raggio.

So often in life, we come into a situation with a list of expectations. Typically, these are private expectations that are not vocalized. For example, when you go out to eat at a restaurant, you expect to pay money to be served the food of your choice. And the servers at the restaurant have the expectation that they will take an order and that the kitchen will make it in a timely fashion so that they can meet their customer's expectations.

There is no special policy or arrangement per se, but there is a societal norm around expectations that we generally agree to.

If you go to a restaurant and they're out of your favorite dish and the server decides to bring you something else without asking, or the food takes hours to make in the kitchen and the server doesn't communicate to you what's going on, expectations aren't met. When this occurs, disappointment and its close friends, anger, frustration, and even rage, often flare up.

Let's use this formula on a discussion of company culture. I'll even use a real example from my own experience.

For our long-term clients, we offer a bundle of one-on-one values alignment coaching hours for their team members to take advantage of when they could benefit from some additional support. The expectations on my end are that they are scheduled in a timely fashion, that we each show up and end on time, that clients have psychological safety to speak their truth and be heard, and that they're coached from where they are now, not where they need to be. Pretty simple expectations, right?

Wrong! With one of my clients, we rolled out a pilot program that involved coaching a group of their leaders. I had asked the team coordinating the efforts to allow me to see the email that went out to ensure that it was worded in a way that accurately described the expectations for the experience. I also asked that we sync up our timing of the communication.

Well, I had been 100 percent unclear because that expectation of mine was broken. An email went out without my approval. And because of this extensive back-and-forth (over one hundred emails later—I wish I were kidding), the scheduling process resulted in days' worth of time spent cleaning up and straightening out.

I was frustrated and disappointed that this agreement wasn't seen through.

But here's the thing: Many of my expectations were in my head. I had thought they would follow through on showing me the email and *then* I would talk to them about the coordination of the schedules. When that first step was skipped, it triggered a domino effect of disappointment because I hadn't articulated my expectations more clearly.

In their minds, they were meeting expectations by getting the communication out. In my mind, they were breaking expectations by not coordinating with me.

Permission to be human. If the people you're working with are stressed out, overwhelmed, or anxious, it's very easy for expectations to go unheard simply because they are trying to survive versus being thoughtful about how they go about accomplishing their work. This is at the core of whether values can be lived. Investing energy into values-based mindfulness practices (more on this in chapter 9) to enable your teams to slow down will get you much further ahead in the short and long term. Otherwise, you'll constantly have the same disappointments.

This kind of disconnect and the frustration that follows happen all the time. We assume that others know what we expect instead of being direct and transparent from the get-go. It's our job as leaders to ensure that our values are never assumptions and that we are direct and transparent with our expectations in how they are lived.

Creating Your Value Promises

There is a distinct difference between being and behaving. You can fully identify as being something but still not behave in a way that reflects that quality. For instance, you might be curious about something but not ask any questions. You could deeply care about racial equity but look the other way when you see a person of color experiencing injustice in front of you. See the difference?

You want to be clear to your team members what expectations there are for both being and behaving in alignment with your values. Enter value promises, your cocreated code of conduct. You develop these statements by asking the following questions of yourself:

- What are the standards and expectations around how people will behave in alignment with our core values?

- What are the promises we can agree to keeping around our behavior for each of our values? What are the shadows or pitfalls to these expectations?

- What might be possible if we live this way?

Permission to be human. Promises can easily be broken, even with the best intentions. As humans, we're going to have bad days, we're going to mess up and not be able to do it all every day. So let's honor that, recognize that it's a real thing, and make plans accordingly to get back on track. Otherwise, you're assuming that no one will stumble, and therefore there's no agreed-upon game plan for getting back up when things fall out of place.

Keeping that in mind, let's go through the framework:

Value: Start with selecting one value that includes your company's personal definition. Use that definition as the lens for creating actionable promises for that specific value.

Promise: One sentence of the specific behavior or action that's expected of every employee in order to honor the stated value.

Pitfall: What is a likely reason someone would not be able to keep that promise, a way this might be misinterpreted or taken advantage of?

Accountability: How can you hold yourself and others lovingly accountable for getting back on track?

Possibility: When this promise is kept, what possibilities does it ignite for your organization?

I've had the honor of going through this very exercise for each of the past four years with the newest cohort of graduate students in Loyola University's Emerging Leaders Master of Business Administration program. It's been a gift to be able to educate students on the value of values and how to make them more than a poster on the wall. Each time we go through the exercise, I see light bulbs going off in their heads as they realize that they have the power to operationalize their values into the cultures that they're a part of. Although I'm not a full-time teacher at the university, I feel the same level of pride as a tenured professor would knowing that they're more equipped to understand and lead these conversations when they start their own businesses or become leaders within other organizations.

Here's a sample from a team of Loyola Emerging Leaders MBA graduate students who were developing their values for their program.

- True friendship: Someone who you can trust wholeheartedly and have emotional reciprocity with.

    - Promise: We promise to consider each other's emotions and thoughts when communicating, no matter whether the situation or actions needed are constructive or affirming.

    - Pitfall: When you're close to somebody, it hurts more when trust is broken.

    - Accountability: Ask the question and discuss. "Do we have each other's best interests in mind?" or "Do we understand where each one of us is coming from?"

    - Possibility: If we're able to be truthful with one another, we will have stronger relationships throughout the program.

- Achievement: To successfully reach a goal or objective through effort, hard work, and cooperation to gain a sense of fulfillment.

  - Promise: We promise to always put forth our best effort.

  - Pitfall: Members can be unmotivated and lack the communication skills necessary to achieve our goals.

  - Accountability: Make sure that everyone is aligned with the goals by establishing them in the beginning and having ongoing check-ins.

  - Possibility: If we successfully come together and all understand each other, then we will achieve our goals.

- Growth: The continuous process of improvement through the contribution of team effort in order to reach a higher level of development.

  - Promise: We promise to consistently set high expectations, remain motivated, and stay determined to achieve greater outcomes.

  - Pitfall: If you are feeling comfortable with or doubtful about your current success, you may not strive for greater achievement.

  - Accountability: Ask yourself, "How can I personally be better?" Or ask your teammates, "What is the next step to improvement?"

- Possibility: If we are able to grow, we will be able to achieve success academically and professionally.

When you go into promises, accountability, pitfalls, and possibility, you're addressing the internal culture. The product of this exercise is essentially your code of conduct (or perhaps you may consider it your values statement or guiding principles). Unlike the definitions of your values, this is not something that typically would go on the website or be broadcasted widely. It might, however, be appropriate to share in your external recruitment efforts. Generally speaking, these statements are for the internal team, and they serve as your agreements to yourself and as your agreements to one another when it comes to how you're going to show up in the behaviors around a given value.

As was the case when you were finalizing your value definitions, value promises are something that can be created in small value groups, then presented to the organization at large for feedback and adjusted accordingly. This can be done as a team with live discussion and facilitation of changes in real time. Or if you have a larger team, it may be more effective to use the same framework Values Connection Survey as suggested in chapter 5:

- Can we commit to this value promise?

- Does this reflect what we stand for?

- Will this promise improve and/or build on positive cultural norms?

And, once again, include an open text box for any additional feedback. As before, these are a yes or no response. Once you have the results in, revisit any of the promises one by one until most team members are in agreement. And just like before, if you don't have majority agreement, go back to the drawing board with the team that created the original promises, review the feedback, and see what alterations need to be made.

This is also a key time to tap into the expertise of your HR team to ensure that you can hold people accountable to these measures in things like hiring, performance reviews, and terminations. Although it might be a really nice idea for team members, it may not be feasible to pull off in your operations. Make sure that it is passed through all the levels of approval before presenting the value promises to your team as options to vote on and finalize.

As before, once they are finalized, it's time to share, celebrate, and begin to consider how you can ensure that these are digestible and integrated into the cultural norms.

Finalized Value Promises

Although the previous exercise is a great way to have your team activate their conscious leadership skills, it's also helpful to create a more simplified version so that team members can keep it at their fingertips. I've had clients create pocket-size printouts, screen savers, desk posters, and wall hangings that reiterate the specific promises each team member is committed to. You get to choose what's right for your team.

Here's an example of what a paired down value promises document could look like:

At this organization we promise to...

- Be open to constructive criticism and offer support when expectations are not met. (accountability)

- Break down silos and increase innovation by involving those who have expertise in the work or a stake in the outcome. (collaboration)

- Provide transparency by explaining our actions through clear communication, including using a common language that applies to all stakeholders. (community)

In this format, it becomes more of pledge, a commitment, a clear set of expectations that is distinct and digestible. What do you think makes the most sense for your company? Share your ideas with your team and go with what would be most effective for them.

Heart-Centered Accountability

In the words of Tamara Renaye, "Accountability feels like an attack when you're not ready to acknowledge how your behavior harms others."[28] With that in mind, we must foster cultures in which people present and receive accountability feedback openly, not defensively. What do you do when a promise is intentionally or unintentionally broken?

Let us consider how to hold people lovingly (instead of fearfully) accountable. The energy that we use to tell ourselves and others that something is offtrack plays a big role in how we get back on track. If you're being guided into place by fear, you're breeding a culture of fear. If you're being guided into place by love, you're breeding a culture of love.

Although I can appreciate the influence of terse and powerful feedback in circumstances that are high stakes, there's almost

---

28 Tamara Renaye (@tamararenaye), Twitter, January 17, 2019, 8:46 a.m., https://twitter.com/tamararenaye/status/1085941440759455749?lang=en.

always another way to communicate and relay your feelings. Fear-based leadership is bound to ignite guilt, shame, and a depletion of confidence. None of those things serve your people in making your company's vision a reality.

In *Dare to Lead*, Brené Brown shares the following:

> Empathy and values live in the contours of guilt, which is why [empathy is] a powerful and socially adaptive emotion. When we apologize for something we've done, make amends, or change a behavior that doesn't align with our values, guilt—not shame—is most often the driving force.

> We feel guilty when we hold up something we've done or failed to do against our values and find they don't match up. It's a psychologically uncomfortable feeling, but one that's helpful. The discomfort of cognitive dissonance is what drives meaningful change. Shame, however, corrodes the very part of us that believes we can change and do better.[29]

Phew! I told you that values work was deep work!

Permission to be human. The first act of living your value promises will be teaching yourself and your people that it's possible to fall on your face and get back up. It is OK to not be perfect and to learn from the imperfections. You can hurt someone's feelings unintentionally and learn how to communicate more effectively in the future. The key is to keep going. Just because it wasn't a picture-perfect conversation the first time doesn't mean that you

---

29 Brown, 129.

don't have a second (or even a twenty-second) chance to do better. Take responsibility where you can, apologize if necessary, and put it into your personal growth tool kit.

Because this is such a big muscle to strengthen and most people don't know where to start, our organization offers an entire soft skills track of training. We do this after the value promises are established to intentionally and precisely guide team members in living these powerful words and giving them the support to reset and realign when they don't. A simple survey that asks team members to anonymously evaluate themselves in how often they keep each value promise (never, sometimes, always) will allow you to quickly point to where the greatest opportunities and proven practices exist. We always start with the greatest opportunities and strategically work our way up. For example, if an entire team is saying that they only sometimes "provide transparency by explaining your actions through clear communication, including using a common language that applies to all stakeholders," then that's a great place to invest in coaching and training on how to be more transparent and thoughtful in both internal and external communication.

Holding people lovingly accountable typically resonates on the surface, but it is much harder to implement when you've never experienced or given that form of feedback. It's a practice to strengthen within all your relationships, and it is great to start with folks you know, love, and trust so that you can learn what it feels like when you do it correctly as well as when you fumble through it.

Using the example from the section on Expectations − Agreement = Disappointment about email communication with coaching clients, let's consider what loving accountability might sound like:

I'd like to debrief with you on the scheduling process for the flow of future coaching sessions. One of your core values is work-life balance, so I know how important it is that we create the sense of ease and grace in our partnership. I really appreciate your diligence in getting it out, and I wanted to loop back on what we can do differently to streamline the coordination moving forward. When are you free for us to talk it though?

This is what fearful accountability sounds like:

Why didn't you check in with me before this email went out? Did you miss my instructions on this process? Now I have over one hundred emails to comb through, and I'm wasting so much more of my time because you didn't do what I expected you to do. I mean, seriously, man, what happened?

How do you get into your heart space before providing loving accountability? It starts with conscious self-awareness and understanding your own energy around the issue. Is your intention to make them feel the pain that you feel? Or is your intention to create the space to be heard and to meet expectations together in the future? It can be hard to decipher where you are in the heat of the moment. In those cases, it's always a best practice to give yourself twenty-four hours to respond. Then tune in to your feelings and emotions, and once you are in a place where you truly want both you and the other person to be better as a result, you can then approach the conversation. You might also appreciate the heart-centering practice that's outlined in chapter 9.

Permission to be human. If you're a newbie at this and want to practice, be vulnerable and authentic about it. You might even say, "I'm in the process of learning how to hold people lovingly accountable. I'm not sure that I know how to do it yet, but I would really appreciate it if you'd be open to growing with me. I want us to be on the same page with meeting expectations, and I want it to feel good between us when we have these conversations. I'm open to your feedback on how it lands with you. Does that work for you?"

The more humanity you show to others through your own journey in growth, the more willing others will be to do the same in their own lives. You can learn even more about these notions in chapter 7, especially the concept of intent before content.

What happens when someone breaks a value promise? Who is holding them accountable if they're not? What kinds of trainings or support have you put into place so that people know *how* to hold people accountable from a place of loving-kindness?

Most humans don't know how to hold people accountable from a place of strength, compassion, and empowerment because most of us are never taught how to do so. If you didn't see it modeled in your life or if you didn't have someone coaching you, wanting the best for you and supporting that growth, then it's highly unlikely that you know how to put these into practice once they're out there in the world.

I often say that if someone doesn't know how to give their loved ones constructive feedback or to set a clear boundary with them, then it's highly unlikely that they know how to do it with their team members at work. Why? Because in many cases, we must learn with people who aren't going to give up on us or write us off right away when we start giving that feedback and don't yet have self-awareness about how we're coming across.

For example, when I first talked to my husband about how annoyed I was by the mess he'd leave on the bathroom sink after he got ready in the morning, I came across as someone who was really pissed off. "Do you not see how disgusting this is? How can you leave the sink covered in all this mess and just go about your day? This makes me want to gag every time I see it. Don't you care about how this impacts me?"

Do you think he took that feedback well? Not at all. Over time he was able to articulate to me how badly I made him feel when I talked to him that way, including my tone of voice and energy. We had a conversation about why his behavior was such a trigger for me and how we could lovingly be more accountable for and thoughtful of each other's needs.

Prior to gaining that self-awareness and realizing how my energy was harming him, I never really checked myself before getting frustrated with team members who were not meeting my expectations. I may not have been as blatantly rude as I was to my husband, but I didn't have empathy or a sense of personal alignment with and grounding in my values when I'd go in to make my point. Without realizing it, I would use shame ("you are bad") and guilt ("you did something bad") to try to meet my needs.

Although I can still have a day where things don't come off as I intended, overall I feel a massive shift in knowing what I need to do to take care of myself before I go into holding someone else accountable for value promises being broken. And that came when I invested in my inner work.

Think about how you're holding yourself accountable. Are you kind to yourself when you're not moving at the pace you expected to be? Are you generous when your body is tired and you simply can't produce in the way you had hoped? Do you say mean things to yourself in your mind when you're not perfect? Or do you give yourself grace?

Personally, this has been one of my greatest journeys and opportunities in life. I often suffer from bouts of imposter syndrome, not-enoughness, and guilt-fueled motivation. Even while writing this book, I've had several experiences of feeling like everyone's going to find out what a phony I am, that I am not worthy of being an author, or if I didn't get one more chapter written within my self-imposed deadline, then I would engage in self-punishment by reminding myself what a loser I was. How friggin' productive is that? That is the definition of fearfully holding someone accountable.

Agreements with Ourselves

Consider don Miguel Ruiz's four agreements:

- Be impeccable with your word.

- Don't take anything personally.

- Don't make assumptions.

- Always do your best.[30]

If we were to each do these four things in regard to ourselves every day, life would be filled with a heck of a lot more love, and we'd truly be able to hold ourselves and others lovingly accountable.

I've been fortunate to travel to Mexico and study with the Ruiz family to learn the Toltec traditions and dive deeper into these four agreements.

---

30 don Miguel Ruiz, "The Four Agreements," accessed May 18, 2005, https://www.miguelruiz.com/the-four-agreements.

don Miguel talks about the inner judge that lives inside of our minds. Constantly criticizing us and others for what things should or shouldn't be. Constantly making us feel not enough and destined to fail. It's when we notice that judge, recognize its voice, and then help it to see its way out that we can finally be free.

When I notice these tendencies popping up now, I am significantly more loving to myself, often responding to that inner judge with things like, "OK, I hear you, and you're just my fear talking. I am doing my best. I am enough. And I know I have a choice in what I believe about myself." I often end with my go-to mantra: "One step at a time, without judgment of pace."

Consider the ways that you can begin to shift in your inner world so that you can massively transform your outer world. Will you start with being vulnerable with a loved one? Asking for a candid conversation with a colleague? Or perhaps looking in the mirror to see how you can be more lovingly accountable to yourself? Meet yourself where you are and take the first microstep toward a new possibility.

Expectations + Agreement = Satisfaction

The value promises process consists of creating clearly defined expectations. Your team is saying, "These are my expectations on how I will behave and how my colleagues will behave when it comes to how we accomplish our work together."

The promise is the expectation. The group conversation or survey with feedback around each one of these promises is where the agreement comes from. When someone reads the promise out loud, we take the time to run it through our personal filters, and we say, "Yep, I agree. Let's move forward with that." Or "No. I have changes that are needed for me to agree."

Remember that you're likely never going to reach 100 percent agreement across the board. It's about getting the vast majority to agree—instead of just the people who are willing to speak up. That's why a survey can be a great tool for ensuring that everyone weighs in. You can always do a combination of the two depending on your current norms and what makes sense for your team. Whatever direction you choose, it is important to create the space and time for discussion and feedback so that things can continue to be molded.

More often than not, these types of behavioral agreements aren't created by an entire organization. They are created by a few people who sit around a table and make decisions for everyone because it's faster and easier to do it that way. Yet this latter process is also how to almost guarantee what people will be talking about around the watercooler and feeling pissed that they're expected to do things they never agreed to.

The whole point of the value promises exercise is that the entire team gets to be a part of creating expectations and then agreeing on them—not feeling coerced or caught off guard but instead feeling considered, empowered, and appreciated. It's extraordinary what happens when you create space for voices to be heard, when you truly listen. Plain and simple: People invest in what they create. That's exactly what we're doing here.

Expectations + Agreement = Satisfaction

Do you see how the value promises create a specific set of expectations for each value? There's no guesswork on how they should be interpreted.

If you choose to do this as a guided conversation in a retreat or meeting setting, be sure to have a skilled facilitator leading the conversation. This can be a member of your team as long as they are a culture keeper and someone people respect within the organization at large. We want to avoid the feelings or experiences of favoritism or bias coming from the facilitator so that you can truly activate possibility for everyone.

When you cocreate your value promises in this way, you'll get so much further ahead.

> If you need support in facilitating that transformational experience, reach out to our team through our website.

If you haven't noticed, this work lights us up and activates an immense sense of purpose for us and for those we work with.

Whatever you choose, do it with intention, integrity, and commitment to the bigger picture: creating a values-driven workplace culture so that your business and its people can thrive.

Values Alignment Review

1. When your team's behaviors (and especially those of the leaders) model your values, others will follow. When the day-to-day exchanges are aligned with what you publicly declare, authenticity is the result. When they do not, distrust and toxicity spread.

2. There is a distinct difference between being and behaving.

3. Value promises create clearly defined expectations. Your team is saying, "These are my expectations of how I will behave and how my colleagues will behave when it comes to how we accomplish our work together."

4. The first act of living your value promises will be teaching yourself and your people that it's possible to fall on your face and get back up. It starts with self-awareness and understanding your own energy around the issue.

5. Most humans don't know how to hold people accountable from a place of strength, compassion, and empowerment because most of us are never taught how to do so.

This chapter highlighted our Values Retreats for teams.

If that opportunity sparked your interest, learn more at www.permissiontobehuman.co, or check out the SparkVision Resources section of this book.

CHAPTER 7

How to Integrate Values into Cultural Norms

It's not hard to make decisions once you know what your values are.
—Roy E. Disney

Troy LeMaile-Stovall, the CEO of TEDCO—Maryland's state-backed incubator of innovation and entrepreneurship—has written, "Core values serve as a lighthouse to help us individually and collectively navigate difficult times and decisions. Like a lighthouse for ships at sea, they expose dangerous paths and provide safe passage to our destination. That passage may not be the most expedient or easiest and may even involve some risk, but it should avoid things that could cause a shipwreck. The lighthouse serves as the 'unwavering guide' that must be followed to avoid disaster."[31]

Just as the most powerful function of a lighthouse is to guide clear passage again and again, core values are felt most deeply when they inform daily practices. Now that you know your values, and you have owned them through your value promises, it's time

---

31 Troy LeMaile-Stovall, "Core Values: Your Unwavering Guide," I95 Business, October 14, 2020, https://i95business.com/articles/1564.

to embrace them as your trusted lighthouse and truly live them. Thus far, everything has resided in the this-is-a-nice-idea category. Even if you take a whole year to find the right words to describe your values and meticulously get all the definitions, promises, pitfalls, accountability, and possibilities nailed down, they don't mean anything unless you live them. They are concepts, not yet practices. Now it is your turn to bring them to life within the many forces and aspects of workplace culture.

This ownership step makes them real. Everything else sets the stage for this moment of implementation and integration. The way you conduct a meeting, the way you speak to clients, the way you engage with your colleagues around a project—these are all opportunities to live your values. You can even create recognition and rewards around them.

If you're not thinking about, integrating, and operationalizing your values, you're inadvertently working against yourself. On the other hand, when you intentionally know, own, and live your values through values filter decision-making, meetings, team dynamics, coaching, one-on-ones, recognition, and celebration, your whole business thrives.

Values Filters

Decision-making can be an extremely difficult and exhausting experience when you're unsure which direction is the "right way" to go. Most of us humans go around and ask loads of other people what they would do in our situation or even hand over decision-making to someone who's higher up because there's a fear of getting it wrong and the consequences that would follow. There's even a term called *decision fatigue*:

> Decision fatigue occurs when people feel exhausted from making too many choices. Psychologists have found that even though we generally like having choices, having to make too many decisions in a short amount of time may lead us to make decisions that are less than optimal.[32]

One of the most powerful aspects of knowing, owning, and living our values is making values-aligned and grounded decisions with total clarity. When we put our questions through a values filter, we can quickly choose what would be in or out of alignment. Once again, it doesn't have to be complicated; it can be supersimple while being simultaneously profound.

Values filters are essentially a handcrafted list of ten questions that have yes or no answers for each value. To move forward with something, you need to get a hard yes on at least eight out of ten questions. This way, you are making a conscious, informed, and intuitive choice on whether it's worth the energy required to move forward or whether you should let it go. A few years ago, I saw Mama Gena, world-renowned author and leader of the School of Womanly Arts, on stage in New York City, and one of her catchphrases has stuck with me ever since: "If it's not a *hell yes*, then it's a *f— no!*" Although you may not use that exact language in the workplace, this is an idea of how you should feel before making your decisions.

Want to better understand whom it makes sense to collaborate or partner with? Whether a new client will be a good fit? If you should invest in a new program or piece of technology? If your candidate is the right choice for the team? Values filters can take

32 Elizabeth Hopper, "What Is Decision Fatigue? Definition and Examples," ThoughtCo., February 29, 2020, https://www.thoughtco.com/decision-fatigue-4628364.

the decision fatigue out of the picture and lead you to the most aligned choice with a sense of confidence and grace.

Crafting Values Filter Questions

When you're creating a values filter, you want to keep two things in mind: Make sure that you phrase the questions in a way that suggests that you *want* to get a yes. For example, you would ask the question "Does this prospect believe in authenticity?" (yes = move forward) versus "Is this prospect inauthentic?" (yes = don't move forward). Be sure that getting a yes equates to the positive aspect of being a good fit and moving forward with that choice. And ensure that the questions are framed consistently throughout so that you don't have to decode them later.

Second, make sure that these are questions that support both the internal *and* the external culture. You can have a stellar internal culture and then bring on a client or partnership that makes the internal team feel crazy. Or you might have an awesome client, but your internal team truly can't support their needs because your team members are so out of alignment with themselves and one another.

Here's a perfect example: Your team is fabulous at communication (it's one of your core values, after all), and they're constantly looping folks in and providing regular updates on status. But your client barely responds to email, seems to constantly be running late to or is unavailable for weekly check-in calls, and rarely gives you the information you need to finish the task at hand by the deadline. There emerges a tug-of-war between expectations and agreements that leads to a consistent feeling of disappointment.

Imagine if you could sniff that out before you agreed to work together. And imagine how much more successful you'd be if you chose not to work with customers, clients, or partners who didn't share your core values.

Beware of the Scarcity Mindset

Categorically avoiding those who do not share your core values may seem extreme and unrealistic, but that's the scarcity mindset working on you—"We *have* to work with the a-holes because they pay our bills," or "We don't have a choice when it comes to whom we can and can't work with; that's a luxury we can't afford."

Permission to be human. If any of that rings a bell, then take a moment to go deeper within yourself and figure out when you started to believe your and your team's well-being were less important than money. Usually, these are deeply ingrained beliefs (from our parents, mentors, competitors, and others) that don't go away simply because you read a paragraph about them in a book.

If this applies to you, I'd encourage more loving curiosity within yourself. I spent three years of my life intentionally healing my relationship with money. After I finally felt like it was available to me and I deserved it, my business tripled, my husband left his societally praised, stable job in finance to work with me, and our life opened up to true authentic possibility, rooted in love and not fear.

Now, it's not all rainbows and sunshine. The moments of insecurity, fear, scarcity, and uncertainty still bubble up at times. But because I've done the deep work around those feelings, I can guide myself off that ledge and come back into alignment with my values and truest self—knowing that what's supposed to be, will be.

Sample Values Filter Questions

Keeping those two significant factors in mind, here's an example of the way I've used a values filter to determine whether a prospective client is a good fit:

1. Does this client value my expertise, and are they willing to invest accordingly? (accountability, inner harmony)

2. Are they able to relate to and connect with my authenticity? (authenticity, vulnerability, empathy)

3. Are they willing to work within my available time frame and respect my time? (inner harmony, accountability, empathy)

4. Are they truly invested in making a change? (transparency, empathy)

5. Do they respond and engage in a timely fashion? (accountability, inner harmony)

6. Are they transparent and willing to show their weaknesses? (transparency, vulnerability)

7. Do they want/are they willing to be held accountable? (accountability, vulnerability, transparency)

8. Do they know their people and believe that their people are the key to success? (empathy, authenticity)

9. Are they willing to be open and honest about their shortcomings? (vulnerability, authenticity, transparency)

10. Does the work we complete together make a true impact? (authenticity, inner harmony)

Here's an example of how you could use a values filter to determine whether you should allocate finances or a budget to a new opportunity based on the values of growth, well-being, community, honesty, and social justice:

1. Does this investment support the growth of our people? (growth)

2. Will our organization grow and expand as a result of this investment? (growth)

3. Does this investment support the well-being of our people? (well-being)

4. Will our organization feel more stable or at ease as a result of this investment? (well-being)

5. Will this investment support our sense of community within our team? (community)

6. Does this investment support our sense of community with our clients? (community)

7. Is this an investment that we'll openly share and feel proud of? (honesty)

8. Does this investment feel in alignment with what we're currently prioritizing? (honesty)

9. Are we able to make this investment without taking away from others? (social justice)

10. Is this investment supporting people who are underserved? (social justice)

And here's the thing—you don't *need* to have ten questions. You might just have one. For example, asking yourself, "Does this align with our core values?" could be simply and completely enough.

Or if you wanted to separate them but still keep it simple, it could look like this:

1. Does this align with our value of growth?

2. Does this align with our value of well-being?

3. Does this align with our value of community?

4. Does this align with our value of honesty?

5. Does this align with our value of social justice?

Imagine that you and your team use this framework every time a little or big decision comes up. Imagine the stress, fear, confusion, and debate that will be eliminated when you agree that decisions must align with your values. Imagine the confidence, independence, sense of possibility, and alignment that will be ignited as a result of this intentional process becoming ingrained in your team's way of showing up every day. *Pretty darn cool, right?*

Infusing Core Values into Meetings

One of the cornerstones of most organizations lies within their ongoing meetings and the team dynamics that do or do not support their values. It's incredible how a meeting can either unite people toward a shared mission or polarize people into their own silos. If you've ever worked anywhere that had meetings, you know what I'm talking about.

There are meetings with formal agendas, well-thought-out presentations, and engaging conversations that move the needle forward. And then there are meetings with no apparent agenda (written or thought of), presentations that are scattered at best, and conversations that go in circles. A company's culture is largely reflective of how people respect one another's time and energy. The team dynamics in meetings are a huge opportunity to observe and determine what else might be possible.

Now imagine a well-thought-out, productive, and engaging team meeting that also wove in the company's values—in other words, a team meeting that was in alignment with everything your company believed in and stood for. Might that make a positive impact? Might that create an infrastructure for your values to be honored and to flourish?

Uh, yeah!

Here are a few ways that you can integrate proven practices while also incorporating your unique core values into team meeting dynamics—in other words, small shifts that are sure to make a big impact.

Meeting Dynamics

Meetings are such a significant part of the day-to-day culture at work. And just as is the case with everything else, some meetings leave us feeling drained and others leave us feeling energized. At the height of the COVID pandemic, online meetings became one of the only ways to connect consistently, but they sadly left most people feeling like Zoom zombies. An in-person meeting that lacks engagement, focus, and connection sucks. And an online meeting that lacks engagement, focus, and connection can suck you dry. Imagine what could be possible if your team looked forward to meetings, connected and built trust during your meetings, and left feeling a sense of purpose and renewed energy when the meeting concluded?

These tried-and-true practices will get you and your team set up for a culture where meetings are valued and serve everyone who attends.

- **Start and end on time.** Timeliness shows a commitment to respect for each other's needs and ignites clear expectations, consistency, and trust. When you regularly start late or run over on meetings, you're sending the message that their time is not valuable. If this is an issue at your organization, consider adding a formal role of a time-keeper in each meeting. This person can be responsible for keeping the meeting facilitator on track with each item on their agenda. Ask facilitators to provide the timekeeper with their agenda and the time allotted for each section in advance so that they can be sure to gently let the facilitator know that it's time to move onto the next agenda item and/or decide as a team if they want to stay on that topic and adjust the meeting or put a pin in it until next time. A timekeeper is especially helpful for giving a five-minute warning to ensure that wrap-up begins as well as a reminder that the time is now complete for when the meeting is slated to end.

This may sound extreme to some who don't have an issue with timekeeping in their cultural norms. But I've been hired to specifically help teams with this issue, and this level of attention to detail and to time has made a huge impact in shifting the norm.

- **Begin with an intention.** Start your meeting explaining why you're together and why it matters. I first heard of this proven practice when Oprah shared that she required meeting organizers to share their intention for the gathering at its start. If the topic or flow of conversation was not in alignment with that intention, the meeting was ended.

With my own work, we ensure that the intention is written at the top of the agenda so that it's loud and clear. Sometimes we even have intentions for different sections of the agenda to ensure that we're transparent with why we're discussing it. Just like with timekeepers and with Oprah's rule, it can be helpful to empower your people to keep you on track with your intentions.

One of my clients uses the phrase "We're in the weeds" whenever a meeting goes down a rabbit hole that it wasn't meant to. Another uses the phrases "Zoom in" or "Zoom out" when they want to remind their team members that they're getting too macro or too micro in their discussions. Having these key phrases developed and agreed upon as an entire company helps others to feel empowered to keep the meeting on track with its intention instead of going completely offtrack and feeling like a waste of time for participants.

- **Recite and review the values.** Take a moment not only to remind yourself of your values but also to pull specific value promises out that apply to meeting norms. When you take the time to honor value promises, people are more likely to behave in alignment with those agreements.

- **Incorporate the values into the agenda.** Are the meeting topics related to your values? Perhaps you're talking about the latest updates to your website, and you also have the values of innovation and growth. Why not make that connection clear instead of relying on a subconscious connection that people may or may not pick up on? I've often broken up meeting agendas into sections based on each value and the content that was connected to it. It made people realize that they were living the values in more ways than they knew, and it demonstrated that living your values didn't have to involve a huge change in what was already happening.

- **Be aware of how the team dynamics are unfolding, and readjust as needed.** Often meetings seem to be going great and then take a sharp turn into rocky territory. Whether it's someone's bad behavior, a poorly organized conversation, or even a meeting that feels like it's redundant or not a good use of time, these are all moments to pause and choose to end a meeting and regroup when things are in a better place. I read a memo that Elon Musk sent to his team around innovation during the pandemic. It stated, "Leave if you're not contributing. Walk out of a meeting, or drop off a call as soon as it's obvious that you aren't adding value. It is not rude to leave; it is rude to make someone else waste their time."

On the other end of the spectrum, what if the meeting is high energy and is getting great engagement? In that case, you may want to check in regarding the availability of your participants, make an agreement together to extend and continue the momentum, or plan to simply revisit the conversation at another time. Please do not assume that people can extend their time with you just because the vibes are high. Check in and act accordingly.

- **Allow others to set boundaries.** Personal and professional boundaries (like value promises) always need to be set and held. Encourage team dynamics that enable them. Consider using prompts like these to get clear on expectations and the boundaries needed around them:

  - What will you/we need to be successful in this project?

  - When do we expect this to be completed?

  - What needs to be reprioritized in order for this to be done with better flow?

  - Considering the last time we took this on, what new boundaries do we need to add in this time in order for us to collaborate more effectively?

  - What is needed to ensure that we have the capacity to take this on?

  - How have we been doing with our value promises together, and where can we get in better alignment with each other?

- **Create space for recognition.** It's always a good rule of thumb to praise more than you criticize. A great way to get in the habit of that is to always hold space for recognition in your meetings, even if they consist of just you and someone else. I once worked at a nonprofit that had shout-outs on the top of the agenda of every meeting. We'd open the floor to anyone who wanted to recognize someone or something. It would sound like, "I want to give Chenire a shout-out for living our value of collaboration. She had my back when I needed assistance seeing the bigger picture. She really helped me to understand what I was missing in order to complete the project."

- **Break into small-group conversations for perspective.** As much as you can, avoid making your meetings feel like lectures. If there's one person talking the whole time, label it properly as a presentation versus a team meeting. Recognize that not everyone feels comfortable with speaking up in real time on the spot, and create experiences that ignite more psychological safety and connection between team members. Whenever appropriate, pause in your meeting and have people turn to those next to them (or put them in online breakout rooms) to provide insight and feedback on the topic at hand. The more you can break up the feeling of a talking head, the more engaged participants will be beyond the meeting itself.

A meeting is most rewarding when participants receive new information from the facilitator and in turn they provide a new perspective on or insight into what was presented. Instead of simply talking at people for your allotted time, what if you instead talked with them about the matter at hand? Consider your usual monthly all-staff meeting where people typically report out the latest in their departments. What might be possible if, after every section, you had a five-minute pair-share with someone about how that information resonated with you and how your team could support its viability? Lots of new possibilities would be ignited because you'd be inviting people to digest and absorb the information instead of just hearing it and moving on.

- **Give permission to be human.** We all have a lot going on in our lives that our colleagues will never know about. When someone is having a bad day or seems off their game, do what you can to check in with them. Something like, "Hey, Cory, I just wanted to check in to see if everything was OK?" can go a really long way if you care about their answer.

One of my former CEOs did just that with me after a team meeting during which he sensed that I was off. Asking me to stay behind, I burst into tears and shared how much I had regretted not going to my uncle's memorial service because it was campaign season and I didn't want to let my team down. He shared his own regrets in his life and empathized with the internal guilt that had been keeping me up at night and unable to focus on my work. Although it didn't take that pain away from me, it gave me permission to be human, seen, and understood.

Coaching and One-on-Ones

As humans, we all make mistakes. We all have days when we wake up on the wrong side of the bed, let our stress out on others, or simply don't have our shit together. No one is immune to those realities. Although we don't want to deny or ignore that fact, we also want to serve as supportive coaches to the people we care about—especially our direct reports.

So many people who are really bad at people stuff get promoted to being managers of others. They got the job because it was the next step up on their growth ladder, but they are not fit to oversee other humans. So many managers are supereffective at building the widget their company makes but really ineffective when it comes to teaching, supporting, and empowering others to build that widget. I've even gone into companies where managers never speak to or meet with their team members because they claim to not have time.

Here's the deal, folks: You don't need to have a weekly hour-long meeting with each individual team member if that's not conducive to being effective in your role. But to truly embrace your humanity, it is important that you have at least a monthly check-in, even if it's for only twenty minutes. Please, schedule these meetings only if you plan to keep them.

One of the most deflating experiences a team member can have is when their manager consistently shows up late, cancels, or simply no-shows for their one-on-ones. Your behaviors send a message, whether intended or not. And when you fall into one of these categories, that message is clear: you are not my priority, your time isn't as important as mine, I don't value your growth, I don't have time to support you.

Yikes! Talk about a way to instantly make people feel like they don't matter.

Let's flip that to look at the possibility that lies within coaching and one-on-ones that are conceived and executed in alignment with your values.

- **Practice value-alignment coaching.** Instead of having your values as a nebulous concept, make them a tool for how you coach your team members. Let's pretend that you had the values of well-being, appreciation, and feedback. In your coaching sessions, you could ask people to rank themselves on a scale of 1 to 10 on how they believe they're doing with living that value and keeping the value promises. From there, you can dig into whichever value or promise(s) that person would like more support with. It's that simple and that complicated all at once. Be sure that you have skilled managers to take on these conversations. If you want to have your managers adopt this practice, ensure that they have the proper training to model these behaviors and support to have these coaching discussions.

- **Spell and pronounce names properly.** This goes with all humans you engage with, but it's especially important with your direct reports. As a two-first-named person, I can't tell you how many times MaryBeth has been written as Marybeth, Mary beth, or even Mary Anne, MarySue, or just Mary. This happens with so many of us. It's not that difficult to see how the person spells their name when they sign off on an email, from which you can copy and paste it into your welcome line of a communication. It's mind-blowing how frequently this disconnect occurs.

Pronouncing someone's name properly is equally key to honoring who that person is. One of my corporate clients has a team member named Renata. Most Americans naturally read her Brazilian name and sound out the *R*. But in her culture, it's a silent *R* that is pronounced as an *H*. What an American might naturally pronounce as Hen-ata.

One day when I facilitated an exercise for the company, we were sharing fun facts about ourselves. When it was her turn, she passively shared that her name was being pronounced wrong but that it was OK and that everyone (inside and outside of work) had done that. Afterward, one team member truly heard her and only pronounced her name as Hen-ata from there on out. A few months later, she joined our culture keepers program and together we began an unofficial campaign to get the entire team to refer to her by her properly pronounced name.

Within weeks of that occurring, she shared with us that it entirely changed her life. Hearing her name properly said back to her every day made her see herself again. So much so that it ignited a health journey and massively changed her overall well-being. She attributed all those changes to being ignited by having one person hear her and show her that she mattered, followed by an entire team doing the same. She shared that it made her feel not only more a part of the company but also more a part of our country. So if you think that pronouncing a team member's name properly isn't a big deal, think again!

- **Assume the best.** You know that old expression? Don't assume because it makes an "ass" of "u" and "me." Get it? It literally spells out what happens when you make assumptions. Nearly every time, we assume the worst about someone or something that's going on. Someone is late to work because they're disrespectful or rude. Another person is on their phone during a meeting and it's assumed that they're disengaged or entitled. What if instead we assumed the best? Perhaps someone is late because they have a lot going on at home and they need some more wiggle room these days, arriving as soon as they're able. Perhaps another person is on their phone because they're live tweeting the recap of the event. Ask for clarity while assuming the best (instead of the worst) in someone.

This was a significant experience for one of my apprentices. He was leading a successful sales team that kicked off with an 8:30 a.m. team huddle every day. That team huddle was a big deal and set the tone for each day. One of his team members started to show up to them late. She mentioned that she was going to be late but didn't explain why. My apprentice came to me sure that he was ready to have a powerful conversation with her. He said that he was going to take her on a walk and get clear with her on expectations. Although she did say that she'd be late, it was not OK to be that late for that many days in a row. He was going to be kind in his delivery and direct with his coaching.

Then I said, "How about if you ask her if she's OK? Didn't you say this is out of character for her?" He shook his head in disappointment, knowing that his approach was too harsh and that his assumptions that she was being disrespectful had taken over his plan of action.

After asking her the next day, she broke down in tears. She shared with him that her father had recently been diagnosed with a brain tumor and that she had moved home to help. The day that she was especially late was because they were missing their cat and discovered that her father had (unknowingly) put him in their refrigerator. This young woman was so scared at the loss of her dad as she knew him and what could have been the loss of her childhood pet. She broke down, releasing the truth that she had been hiding to try to save face in front of her sales role. From that moment on, their relationship changed for the better, and he was able to be a more effective coach and culture keeper by giving her permission to be human.

- **Listen.** All humans want to be heard and to know that what they have to say matters. The only way that can happen is if you listen with the intention to truly hear someone. So much is communicated in forms beyond words. Hearing is something that can happen accidently, involuntarily, or effortlessly while listening is focused, voluntary, and intentional. A skilled listener is paying attention to what you are saying while also interpreting the tone of voice and the body language that accompanies those words. If you can master being a good listener and then show them that they are understood, you will gain an immense amount of trust and loyalty from your people.

- **Share your intent before content.** I heard this expression when undertaking a crucial conversation training many years ago. It was such a powerful tip that I use it practically every day, and it's exactly what it sounds like: Before you share the content of what you have on your mind, share your intention and why it matters to you. This is an especially great tip when it comes to difficult conversations. This might sound like, "Helene, you are one of my top performers on this team. And because of that, I really have to dig deep to find areas of opportunity for you. But I know you're always invested in growing, and these little things will make a big difference in your impact when it comes to living our values. So let's start by celebrating your wins from last week's pitch and also dig in to opportunities with our core values alignment." Or perhaps, "Jordan, you've been such a reliable go-to for this team over the years; it's one of your greatest strengths. That's why I was surprised by the change in your follow-through recently. I'm sure there's more going on behind the scenes than I realize, and I want to support you in the process of getting back in alignment with that strength."

The cool thing about this approach is that it also gets you in check with yourself to understand why this conversation matters to you. And just like with loving accountability, if your intention is not one that's ultimately positive, this is not the time for you to have this discussion—no exceptions. Check your ego and wait until you are in better alignment with yourself before you broach the subject.

- **Provide constructive and affirming feedback.** Most people think that feedback is only about what someone can do better. If a former boss ever said to me, "Hey, MaryBeth, let me give you some feedback," I would immediately brace myself for impact. As you've already read, it's important to share what's going well along with what isn't. It's a proven practice to offer more affirming than constructive feedback whenever it's possible and real (don't make it up). Show your people that you know that feedback is rewarding and not just a dreaded conversation about their shortcomings.

And please, avoid the mistake of the feedback sandwich. Many times, we have been told that if you say a nice thing, followed by an area of improvement, then end with another nice thing that people will be able to handle the constructive feedback more. But that's simply not the case. Remember that negativity bias? Of course we're going to focus on the area of improvement way more. You can give affirming feedback on its own and you can give constructive feedback on its own as long as you use the intent before content structure.

- **Ask permission to give feedback.** Let's be clear: You can always give someone feedback whether or not you have their permission, but when you ask, it will likely go better. It can be as straightforward as, "Hey, Monique, are you open to feedback on last week's event? I'd love to celebrate and support you when you have the capacity for it." That type of phrase is particularly useful if you would like to spend some time with them one-on-one to debrief.

- **Be specific with your feedback.** I heard on a *Radical Candor* podcast, "If you can say it to a dog, it's not real feedback." And that really stuck with me. Think about it. "Good job!" or even "Bad job!" doesn't help anyone. Why? Because you're not taking the time to explicitly tell people what made it good or bad. This is very often the case when things go well. We're so used to pulling out one of our go-to statements, like "Nice work, Jennifer!" or "Really great job there, Abdul!"

Although those words are always nice to receive, they don't provide any direction or guidance for what you'd like that person to keep doing. Think: "Nice work, Jennifer! I really appreciated how you took the time to set a clear intention for everyone when we started and how well you wove our values into your presentation. You were very thoughtful in your process." Or "Really great job there, Abdul! I loved the way that you included that energizing music and shared your personal story with everyone. You really lived our value of connection, and it was cool to get to know you better."

- **Practice two-way feedback.** Most people are used to the executives giving feedback to their team members, and that's that. It's no surprise, as most of our current societal norms are designed around the model of someone being in the power seat and the other being the subordinate. It can be empowering (and maybe even scary at first) for team members to give their managers feedback—especially if this is a change to the existing dynamics.

I'd recommend that you start with something that is tangible and relatable versus asking, "Do you have any feedback for me?" Most team members would be caught off guard and move on quickly with a "Nope—all good here!" in an attempt to keep the peace. Psychological safety is the only way these conversations can happen authentically.

Try something like this: "I really appreciate your perspective, Ganesha, so I'm going to add a new section to our ongoing one-on-ones that includes the opportunity for you to give me feedback. I know that might feel daunting, so I want to be intentional about where we start. How about the next time we meet, you give me one idea on how I can be more effective or impactful with our one-on-ones? It can be anything, big or small, but something that would make you feel like these meetings were an even better use of your energy."

This example recognizes your thought process and the vulnerability it takes for feedback to occur, and it introduces a specific focus to get things started. As you move up in your levels of psychological safety, you could even get to the point where your one-on-ones included two-way feedback around living your values. While you provide them feedback on how they're doing with embodying a certain value, you could then ask them to provide you with the insight from their lens. That conversation may sound like this: "Darren, you're doing an incredible job when it comes to embodying our value of integrity. Just the other day, I saw how you stayed late to support Phyllis on her project to ensure that she met her deadline. I'm really impressed with how much you're doing to keep the whole team, including yourself, in integrity. The next time we meet, I'd really appreciate it if you could provide me with feedback on how I'm doing when it comes to my integrity relative to you. Where am I in alignment, and where are some opportunities for me to do better?"

Taking this approach will significantly differentiate you from most other organizations and will give your team a huge upper hand in creating a loyal and honest culture. It activates values like trust, authenticity, communication, vulnerability, empathy, and growth, to name a few.

- **Choose curiosity.** Curiosity is the cure to all frustration. Whenever you find yourself being ignited by frustration in another team member, do your best to shift up to the energy of curiosity. The majority of the time, you're frustrated based on assumptions that you've made, and you've become the victim of the story you've created about the situation. Be a conscious, mindful leader by pausing and recognizing that you can choose curiosity. You may consider go-to statements and questions like the following:

  - Tell me more about that.

  - Help me understand what happened.

  - I don't want to make any assumptions, so please walk me through your experience here.

  - What do you mean by that?

  - How can we make things right between us?

  - What do we need to discuss first?

- **Make room for grief.** Writing this book during the time of the coronavirus compelled me to expand this section. Pandemic or not, people are often going through cycles of loss. The expression "Everyone you meet is fighting a battle you know nothing about. Be kind. Always." says it all.

Whether it's as heavy as the death of a loved one, or news of an unfounded police killing of a person of color, or even an experience like a trusted team member leaving the company or the loss of funding for a project, grief is something to honor. One of the worst things we can do is push toxic positivity onto them—believing that no matter how dire or difficult a situation is, people should maintain total optimism.

Most of us don't know how to make room for grief in our own lives, let alone encourage or support others to do what they need to be well. Any effort you can make to recognize the complexities that grief brings into our human lives is a big win. Tune in to your own needs and the needs of your team members so that they don't have to pretend that they're OK if they're not.

I became an unintentional pro at this during the first year of my business. Within a six-month span, my team of three experienced the unexpected death of a mother, father, and, in my case, two grandparents. They were huge losses for each of us respectively, and we were all trying to find our way back to ourselves while swimming in a sea of incredible grief. I made sure that they knew that nothing was more essential than them making room for their grief, which included three massively important things:

1. Cancel all nonessential meetings.
2. Make space for self-care every day.
3. (Re)ignite good habits.

Unlike when my father died, at which point I was in a different position professionally, in this case, as the CEO of my own company, I felt like I could control the experience around grief more authentically. We all grieve differently, and most people don't know how to be with or support someone who is moving through and with their pain. And that's OK. You don't have to be an expert in everything. But you do need to recognize the intense human experience of grief.

During one of my ongoing Mindful Minutes series, where we do fifteen minutes of guided mindfulness practices with teams throughout the week, someone I hadn't met before sent me a private message saying how much that session helped her in her grief around the recent loss of her mom. It was my choice whether to engage with her message. And with an open heart, I did and offered to stay on the line with her after the session ended. We wound up talking about the loss of our parents and how we can still get signs from them after they transition. I told her about the book *Signs,* by Laura Lynne Jackson, which massively healed my pain over the loss of my grandparents; based on the book, I knew I could still connect with them through signs.[33]

She immediately shared that dragonflies were the sign from her mom, that every time she saw them, it felt like her mom was present. In just a few minutes of talking about it, an incredible bond and connection was formed between us—someone who I hadn't met prior to this session. In the following weeks, I saw dragonflies regularly and sent her an email to tell her this. She in turn asked me for my favorite colors, and a few months later, a package arrived in the mail. She had knitted me a beautiful set of dragonfly pot holders and a table runner to thank me for making room for her grief and listening to her experience. That

---

33 Laura Lynne Jackson, *Signs: The Secret Language of the Universe* (New York: Dial Press, 2020).

connection between us is now there for a lifetime. And it truly was a matter of minutes of conscious connection.

It's important to note that others can be there and listen, but you will walk down your own path, at your own pace, with your own pain. In the end, grief is a walk alone. You will come to your own peace, in your own time, in whatever way makes sense for you. My experience is not yours, and it is not a suggestion that one size fits all. It's far from that when it comes to loss. But perhaps this can ignite some meaningful ways of approaching your own grief or supporting team members who are experiencing theirs.

- **Use the winning formula: Expectations + Agreement = Satisfaction.** As you read in chapter 6, this is such a clean formula, one that people get right away. I use it in my own coaching on a regular basis. From the start, set clear expectations of what you want your people to accomplish. Make sure that you're in agreement with each other. Then check in on those very expectations during your time together. It's a wonderful framework for your ongoing conversations.

- **Give permission to be human.** These don't seem like massive changes, yet they all are. If you've never given someone thoughtful feedback, held someone accountable, or been comfortable around other people's range of emotions, you know this is big work. There is no expectation that you'll do all these things perfectly every day. Just pick one to start with and master it. See how it gets adopted and where it needs more support. Then move on to incorporating something else. It's not about how quickly you get there; it's about your intention to evolve. One step at a time, without judgment of pace.

Engagement and Retention

Your values can absolutely (and in my humble opinion, should) be *the* way that people feel engaged and therefore stay committed in their roles. But how many organizations harness values in that way?

As you read before, employee engagement is the emotional commitment the person has to the organization and its goals. This emotional commitment means that engaged employees care about their work and their company. They don't work just for a paycheck or just for the next promotion but on behalf of the organization's goals. When employees care—when they are engaged—they will go above the minimum requirements to see something through and do the right thing.[34] Remember all those stats from chapter 6 on the effect of employee engagement on your bottom line?

How can you make sure that your company's practices are aligned with your values when it comes to employee engagement and retention?

- **Be clear to be transparent.** Transparency is a transformative value in itself. It's closely aligned with trust, connection, and communication. As Brené Brown says in *Dare to Lead,*

  > Clear is kind. Unclear is unkind. I first heard this saying two decades ago in a twelve-step meeting, but I was on slogan overload at the time and didn't even think about it again until I saw the data about how most of us avoid clarity because we tell ourselves that we're being kind, when what we're actually doing is being unkind and unfair. Feeding people half-truths

---

34   Kevin Kruse, "What Is Employee Engagement?" *Forbes*, June 22, 2012, https://www.forbes.com/sites/kevinkruse/2012/06/22/employee-engagement-what-and-why/?sh=33404b6a7f37.

or bullshit to make them feel better (which is almost always about making ourselves feel more comfortable) is unkind. Not getting clear with a colleague about your expectations because it feels too hard, yet holding them accountable or blaming them for not delivering is unkind. Talking about people rather than to them is unkind.[35]

- **Respond to emails.** I wish I didn't feel the need to even write this section, but I do. So many executives are so inundated with emails that they get lost, fall to the wayside, and are never addressed. This means that it's time to hire administrative support to ensure that you can reply to emails in a timely and thoughtful fashion. It's frustrating and damaging to team members when they have to hunt you down to get a response. And if you're avoiding the email because you don't feel like dealing with it, you're perpetuating that attitude with other team members.

Even if you need to politely decline or delegate the responsibility of the next steps around the email to someone else, do it with integrity. Don't just hope that person forgets or that they will stop bothering you if you don't get back to them. Treat your team members with the same response time and clarity that you desire to be a cultural norm. And while you're at it, perhaps you want to see which values and their promises you might be breaking by not responding to your emails?

- **Involve more people in decision-making.** Just as you've done with your values and value promises, it's always a good idea to ignite opportunities for feedback and buy-in.

---

35 Brown, 48.

What approach are you taking with decision-making? Are you engaging people who will be affected by the decision or making a choice based on your personal preferences? Are you using your values filter or creating your own system?

- **Respect time off.** This can be one of the trickiest points of all, given our societal norms of go-go-go and always being on. Although the internet has brought us game-changing innovations, it's also steamrolled a lot of boundaries for people and negatively influenced their relationship to their own inner harmony, well-being, and balance. As a leader within an organization, you are constantly sending messages to your team about what's expected through your own behavior. If you're emailing people over the weekend, you create an expectation that they will be checking and responding to you over the weekend. If you must send an email after hours, make sure that you tell people that you don't expect them to respond (if you really don't). The same goes for when you or your people are on vacation. Respect that time, and value it as what's needed for your team member to be able to perform at high levels when they return. In fact, according to Project: Time Off, the majority of working Americans reported the positive effects of taking vacation time and said the following about when they returned to work:

  - Their mood was more positive (68 percent)

  - They had more energy (66 percent) and motivation (57 percent)

- They felt less stressed (57 percent)

- They were more productive (58 percent)

- Their work quality was better (55 percent)[36]

Project: Time Off research also found the following:

- Employees who reported that their company encouraged vacation were much happier with their jobs (68 percent) than those who worked at places where either vacation was discouraged or managers were ambivalent about taking time off (42 percent).

- Employees were also more likely to use all their vacation time (77 percent compared to 51 percent).[37]

So please, take your lunch breaks, your nights, your weekends, your holidays, your paid time off. Leave by example. You are not alive so that you can work every moment of your life. If you embody the values of inner harmony, balance, family stability, or well-being, it will be much easier for team members to follow suit. End work on time, take vacations, and show up to important milestone moments outside of work, even if that means you take a day off. Demonstrate that everyone has the ability to choose by modeling that behavior.

36 American Psychological Association Center for Organizational Excellence, "2018 Work and Well-Being Survey," American Psychological Association, June 2018, http://www.apaexcellence. org/assets/general/2018-work-and-wellbeing-survey-results. pdf?_ga=2.36703840.1500482177.1614039847-994391399.1614039847.
37 Ibid.

- **Volunteer together and apart.** Corporate social responsibility is becoming one of the more common values across the country. Having specific opportunities for your team to take on a volunteer project is one of the best ways to ignite teamwork and team building while simultaneously making an impact in your community. You can even amplify your own workplace values by partnering with a nonprofit that shares your values. This will give team members a whole new way of experiencing those shared values while making a new impact in their community.

Research has shown that volunteer programs improve employee satisfaction, foster employee engagement, and boost retention. For instance, the Macquarie Graduate School of Management found that 93 percent of employees who volunteered through their company reported being happy with their employer, and 54 percent of those who were proud of their company's contributions to society were engaged at work.[38]

It's also empowering to provide volunteer hours for your team members to use as they desire. When I was a fundraiser at a nonprofit, we had a bucket of volunteer hours that we could use each quarter on our own time. It was fantastic because I was a big sister in the Big Brothers Big Sisters program, and there were often experiences that I wanted to support my little sister with that happened during work hours that I could now take advantage of with more grace. I found myself being incredibly grateful for that autonomy while also being celebrated and supported for my personal contributions.

---

38 Lina Caneva, "Corporate Volunteering Improves Employee Engagement—Study," Pro Bono News, September 24, 2013, https://probonoaustralia.com.au/news/2013/09/corporate-volunteering-improves-employee-engagement-study/.

So much so, in fact, that after a few years of being a big sister, my mentee unexpectedly became our foster daughter. It was an emergency situation, and my husband and I knew that we had to step up and have her in our lives in a more significant way. We both let our companies know, and they were fully supportive. To the point that the CEO of my company pulled me aside and said, "I heard what's going on now, and I want you to know that you have full permission and support to do whatever you need anytime you need to for her. Know that we all trust and believe in you. Just let us know what you need, and you'll get it." In that one conversation, all my fears of volunteer hours running out melted away because he gave me full permission to be human.

- **Invest in team building.** Much like volunteerism, investing in time for people to be social and to get to know one another has staggering returns. When you know people for more than just their job title and responsibilities, you organically become more invested in them. This doesn't need to consist of some kind of huge event (although I'm a massive proponent of retreats); it can also be little moments that are integrated into your regular ongoing operations.

I work with a company that began a new way of connecting while everyone was remote during the pandemic. Each morning they have an all-staff check-in call, and they kick it off by having one person share a fun fact about themselves. It's ranged from people sharing music talents, to the inner workings of their man caves, collections of memorabilia, and awards and trophies from the past. The idea was to share something about themselves that their team members likely didn't already know. Something that takes only a few minutes out of the agenda has had an incredible return for everyone on the line. Team members who had been working with each other for years felt more connection and commitment to one another than ever before because they understood who their team members were and what they had in common and appreciated what they had that was distinct. So many sparks went off that ignited more offline conversations as a result of simply asking people to share more of themselves within a specific framework.

- **Be authentic.** This concept of authenticity is so overplayed right now, I know. But the reason we're hearing everyone talk about it is because it's completely connected to people's well-being. We are our most authentic selves when our behaviors, actions, and experiences reflect our core values. That said, being authentic can also sometimes become an excuse for bad behavior.

Bob Burg, Hall of Fame Keynote Speaker and coauthor of *The Go-Giver*, a book about changing the focus of success from getting to giving in business, posted the following on his LinkedIn account:

Authenticity should never be used as an excuse. Like the person who says, "I have anger issues and I yell at people a lot. If I were to stop doing that it wouldn't be authentic of me."

Baloney! It simply means (s)he has an *authentic problem* that (s)he needs to authentically overcome in order to become a better, higher, and more effective authentic version of herself/himself.

In other words, rather than using authenticity as a reason or excuse to stagnate and not improve, use it as motivation to propel you to grow; to step up into your true, much more effective, and higher version of your authentic self.[39]

- **Encourage collaboration.** When people can collaborate in a healthy and productive way, it creates a lightened load for everyone and brings in some of the best innovation you could imagine. That old expression "Two heads are better than one" is almost always true. When people collaborate, something bigger than themselves emerges.

Keep in mind that not everyone likes to collaborate. Although that's not an excuse, it's an opportunity to be more thoughtful about what collaboration could look like. Perhaps someone really dislikes the brainstorming process but deeply enjoys the finishing touches. Bring them in when it's time for them to shine in the collaborative process instead of forcing everyone to be involved in every detail of a collaboration.

Diversity of thought and perspective are so important in the collaborative experience. Diversity comes from so many factors such as race, religion, generation, gender, sexual orientation, ability, economic, neurodiversity, cognitive, and experiential, to name a few. When you have a diverse team, you have a wealth of varied life experiences, which causes individuals to approach problems differently and to empathize differently. So many more people can be touched, served, and moved when you engage in diverse thinking instead of just a like-minded approach.

---

39 Bob Burg, LinkedIn, 2020, https://www.linkedin.com/posts/bobburg_authenticity-growth-sales-activity-6716673254498693120-EFjH.

- **Mentor.** Mentoring is one of the best ways for your team members to feel valued and supported at work. Loyalty, engagement, and retention of team members are often increased a great deal when people have a genuine mentor at work. Keep that word *genuine* in mind when you look at the mentoring relationships (or lack thereof) in your office. I've worked with companies that had a forced mentoring program in which people were required to meet with someone more senior than them at least once a month in order to gain mentorship. Although in theory that's an awesome idea, many of the mentees felt overlooked and unimportant after their mentors regularly canceled, no-showed, or rescheduled at the last minute. Then once they did meet, the mentor was not engaged or actively interested in their mentee's needs.

This example could go the other way too. I've been an assigned mentor to someone who did not seem interested in being mentored by me. It felt like she was mostly coming for the meal I was treating her to and completely relied on me to carry and engage in conversation. That can be an unrewarding situation for both sides.

Consider values mentors. This would completely negate the belief that a mentor is someone with a certain title or credential, shifting focus to the fact that they have mastered the embodiment of a certain value and that they are open and willing to share their wisdom with others who want to grow in that area. This can be very similar to one-on-one coaching.

For example, when a graduate student asked me to be his mentor, we spent time defining and understanding what success would look like for each of us. We then went into understanding the values he wanted to strengthen in his life and compared them to the values that I felt I had reached authentic embodiment of. Then I looked to him to see which values he had embodied that I wanted to strengthen. We landed on my mentorship of the value of inner harmony and his mentorship on the value of adventure. Every time we got together, this was the frame for our conversations. We'd discuss whether our latest experiences were in or out of alignment with our stated values and celebrate and provide wisdom to the other whenever appropriate. It made the typical mentoring experience so much more dynamic and personalized. We cut through the BS and went straight to the good stuff.

This approach may or may not be exciting to others. As with any coaching or mentoring relationship, you want to be sure that there are clear expectations on the front end that you have agreed on so that you can be sure to meet each other's needs.

- **Help them understand how they're making the vision a reality.** When you can connect the dots to the bigger picture, people have a sense of purpose and meaning. Whether you're the person who's emptying the trash bins or the person who's executing the largest projects, each of your team members deserves to know how their piece of the work is adding to the bigger picture. Check out *Start with Why*, by Simon Sinek, if you want to dive more deeply into this topic.[40]

- **Give permission to be human.** If someone is disengaged and/or seems like they're reaching a breaking point in terms of continuing as a part of the team, it's time to have one of those honest conversations. Start with your intention and then ask them what's been going on and

---

40 Simon Sinek, *Start with Why: How Great Leaders Inspire Everyone to Take Action* (New York: Penguin Group, 2009).

what you can do to support them. Most of the time, there's something you can do about it, but sometimes there really isn't. Don't make false promises but rather look at what's in the best interests of that individual and support them accordingly.

Appreciation, Recognition, and Celebration

Appreciation, recognition, and celebration are three of the most powerful and effective ways to keep your employees motivated, engaged, and proud of their impact. Yet they're often overlooked, underused, and even *free* tools that are left sitting on the table. Technically, these concepts could fall under the engagement and retention category. However, they are so significant in the effect that they can create that they're worthy of their own section. Steven Covey, author of the best-selling book *The 7 Habits of Highly Effective People*, states, "Next to physical survival, the greatest need of a human being is psychological survival, to be understood, to be affirmed, to be validated, to be appreciated."[41]

Picture this: Your team sets lofty goals for the year, and one by one, team members are accomplishing them like no one's business. Big wins are happening left and right. As the leader of that team, you do an internal happy dance in salsa mode, and you feel like everything is falling into place. But you're moving so quickly that "celebrating" is simply setting the next goal. So you take a step back to reflect. You look around at your larger team and realize that no one is celebrating with you. You wonder, "Does anyone notice? Does anyone care? Does this even matter?"

---

41 "The Five Languages of Appreciation in the Workplace Quotes," GoodReads, accessed December 1, 2018, https://www.goodreads.com/work/quotes/16185816-the-five-languages-of-appreciation-in-the-workplace-empowering-organiza.

Can you relate? This was my story just a few years ago. I was swimming in wins—but I was also drowning in a work addiction. I never took the time to stop, reflect, and intentionally celebrate the accomplishments that I earned through dedication and tenacity. The people around me couldn't have cared less that I was accomplishing my goals; it was just business as usual.

When we don't take the time to honor our accomplishments, it's almost as if they didn't matter in the first place. Because we are leaders in the workplace, it's our responsibility to celebrate the successes of those around us.

An *Inc.* magazine article noted that "celebrating our accomplishments is critical to our success." The author made three big points to support this argument, which I've summarized here:

1. The act of celebrating changes your physiology and strengthens your psychology. When you celebrate, endorphins are released inside your body and you feel incredible. When you accomplish something and don't take the time to celebrate, you are robbing yourself of an important feeling that reinforces your success.

2. Celebrating strengthens your relationships. Your own celebration is contagious, and those around you want to share in your success. As accomplishments are properly recounted, new ideas and opportunities are formed and shared.

3. Your celebrations attract more success. Success begets more success, so it's only natural to build on existing momentum, especially during events of celebration.[42]

Knowing these facts, I did an informal poll among my network on LinkedIn. I asked, "How do you celebrate when you accomplish a goal?" I received about one hundred responses. Not surprisingly, the majority of folks celebrated with food and drink. But right next to that, people said they set another goal. In my mind, this means that they're rewarding themselves with more work—not celebrating what was accomplished. *Am I wrong?*

We simply don't celebrate enough.

So next time you or someone on your team has a big or a little win, take a moment to recognize the accomplishment and celebrate. Here are a few ways you can do that in alignment with your values:

- **Give a toast.** If every meal or celebration started with a toast to something positive, the world would be a happier place. Taking just a few minutes to raise a glass (with or without alcohol in it) creates good vibes and feelings of shared connection through celebration. If you're hosting a gathering where food is involved, how about you weave in a toast next time? Try something like, "I want to give a toast to our administrative team. You all have been carrying the weight of this recognition program for the past nine months, and our entire company is better off because of your efforts. I learned that we have so much good happening here that we never would have heard about

---

42 Bill Carmody, "3 Reasons Celebrating Your Many Accomplishments Is Critical to Your Success," *Inc.*, August 12, 2015, https://www.inc.com/bill-carmody/3-reasons-celebrating-your-many-accomplishments-is-critical-to-your-success.html.

if it weren't for this process. We must keep this positive momentum going to continue to know, own, and live our values. Cheers to the administrative team for designing and seeing this program through. You are the epitome of what it means for us to recognize how we are and can continue to live our values more deeply."

- **Show gratitude.** Being appreciated goes a long way in igniting positive feelings about and associations with work. And just like giving affirming feedback, giving specific gratitude also goes a long way. Instead of "Thanks for your help today!" you could take it a step further to "Thanks for your help today! It made such a difference to have your perspective and buy-in during this process. We really appreciate you and how intentional you are about living our value of innovation."

A national gratitude survey conducted by Janice Kaplan showed that "grateful people earn about 7 percent more than their ungrateful colleagues. They also experience lower stress, are more resilient and physically fit, have 12 percent lower blood pressure, and simply feel better."[43]

You might even want to consider a team huddle at the start and end of each day during which everyone shares one thing they're grateful for. When we're in the energy of gratitude, more possibility opens up for us. So why not support your team in starting and ending their time with you on a positive note?

- **Create a physical expression of celebration.** Doing happy dances, ringing a bell, or even playing upbeat music to

---

43 Christine Porath, *Mastering Civility: A Manifesto for the Workplace* (New York: Grand Central, 2016), 101.

ignite physical movement is an awesome way to express celebration. It was commonplace in finance for there to be a bell in the sales team's office, and whenever someone made a big sale, they would go over to the bell, ring it, and get high fives from their team members to celebrate that moment. When I worked at a grassroots nonprofit, we'd celebrate the small wins of our students by turning on Miley Cyrus's song "Party in the USA," singing at the top of our lungs, and dancing it out together. Again, one of these may resonate with you more than the others—you must be authentic with your own style and figure out what makes sense for you and for your team.

- **Encourage people to recognize one another.** As related earlier, it's important to create opportunities for people to recognize others who activate your company's core values and shout them out for their efforts. I've also worked with companies that use stationery that's been created specifically to drop off at someone's desk or put in the mail and has a template for the value they want to recognize someone for, what that person did, and how it impacted them.

One company even created a whole I-Spy campaign in which team members and clients could use an online portal to nominate people for living their values. Then at the end of each month, the nominations were collected and one was randomly selected for a prize while everyone got the opportunity to share the good vibes by hearing what folks had submitted.

- **Give awards.** Value awards are pretty darn cool! They can be as complex as having a nomination process with folks reviewing nominees against a standardized rubric for selection. Or if you don't have that capacity, they could be done as a random drawing, as I outlined in the previous I-Spy example. Do what you have the capacity to do most equitably and thoughtfully. The awards could come monthly, quarterly, or annually, an update from the more traditional Employee of the Month type of award. You can choose to add some sort of incentive or not. I've found that prime-location parking spots, gift cards, extra time off, or even company apparel go a long way in helping people feel celebrated. Recognizing that not everyone likes the same things, allow your team members to choose whenever possible.

- **Honor progress and failure.** If you want to ramp up your psychological safety and innovation, start to celebrate failures and see what happens. One of the people I coach came from a company that would throw failure parties, with cakes and everything. The idea was to normalize that everyone fails and that we need to embrace that failure in order to do better in the future. Make note of your progress and celebrate the new wisdom you have for next time.

- **Say thank you, and mean it.** Saying thank you can do double duty as a way to celebrate and recognize someone. Don't be stingy with your appreciation; it costs you nothing to tell someone that you're grateful for their efforts. But be sure that it's not shallow. We want to thank people with depth and quality around why we appreciate them so that they understand what behaviors we'd love to keep experiencing with them.

- **Recognize important dates.** Think first day on the job, birthdays, work anniversaries. When you can remember these dates and make even a tiny effort to recognize them, it can be remarkably rewarding for the person on the receiving end. This can be an annual calendar reminder that you set up so that you can drop a quick email, make a call, or perhaps even take a team member out to lunch to recognize and honor their milestone.

- **Share accomplishments internally and externally.** People get excited for you when good things are happening. And it's not just your team that can benefit from a good vibe boost around sharing those wins. When you take the time to intentionally shout out your accomplishments, with grace, humility, and love, others feel happy too. Next time you send out a newsletter or post on social media, might there be something you could intentionally praise about your team's accomplishments that would ignite that possibility in others? It's worth trying to find out.

- **Incorporate impromptu team huddles.** You know when sports teams get in a huddle, put their hands in the center, and then leave with a "One…two…three…go, team"? Well, that stuff works! It may seem silly to take a practice out of athletes' playbooks, but it's worth trying. Before any big experience my team puts on, we gather in a huddle (whether remote or in person), each share our intentions for the experience, and then honor them by ringing an energy chime (a simple bell that emits an extended calming sound) and just breathing into those intentions together. It's not quite the sports approach, but it's another example of how you can make a concept like a team huddle reflect your own values.

- **Give permission to be human.** Remember that one size does not fit all when it comes to how people like to celebrate or feel appreciated. For some people, making a big staff announcement about how much you appreciate them would be a great joy, and for others that could feel embarrassing. Check in and find out how people like to be recognized and then respect what's right for them. Something that might be the highlight of your life might feel like a punishment to someone else.

Appreciation, recognition, and celebration go a very long way in connecting us to our purposes and making us feel good in life. Gary Chapman explains in *The Five Languages of Appreciation in the Workplace*, "When relationships are not nurtured by a sense of appreciation, the results are predictable:

- Team members will experience a lack of connectedness with others and with the mission of the organization.

- Workers will tend to become discouraged, feeling 'There is always more to do and no one appreciates what I'm doing.'

- Often employees will begin to complain about their work, their colleagues, and their supervisor.

- Eventually, team members start to think seriously about leaving the organization and they begin to search for other employment."[44]

With these crucial factors in mind, what will be your first step toward igniting more intentional appreciation, recognition, and celebration in your culture on an ongoing basis? How can you shift these things from being special occasions to being a part of your everyday norms? What might be possible in your business if every day people felt the power of connection and belonging through appreciation, recognition, and celebration?

Consider all the ins and outs of your workplace culture; where might you be able to be more impactful with linking your core values to daily interactions? Have you considered your decision-making processes, meeting dynamics, engagement and retention? Are you digging deeper, or are you just grabbing for the easiest, fastest box-checking practices? The more you reflect on where your values are at present and how they can be further infused into the workplace, the more successful you and your team will be in connecting them with your conscious and subconscious thinking, planning, and leadership approaches. And the more your team makes those connections, the more everyone has the opportunity to grow in alignment with their greatest potential—instead of being stuck in how it's always been done before. The more you reflect, the more you connect, the more you grow! Cheers to that opportunity and the possibility that lives inside it when you choose the path of your values.

---

44 "The Five Languages of Appreciation in the Workplace Quotes."

Values Alignment Review

1. The way you conduct a meeting, the way you speak to clients, the way you engage with your colleagues around a project—these are all opportunities to live your values.

2. A company's culture is largely reflective of the extent to which people respect one another's time and energy. The team dynamics in meetings are a huge opportunity to observe and determine what else might be possible.

3. Praise more than you criticize.

4. Intent before content. Before you share the content of what you have on your mind, share your intention and why it matters to you.

5. Appreciation, recognition, and celebration are three of the most powerful and effective ways to keep your employees motivated, engaged, and proud of their impact.

CHAPTER 8

How to Integrate Values into Operations

Don't tell me what you value; show me your budget,
and I'll tell you what you value.
—Joe Biden

I magine if your company only hired people who were already intrinsically motivated by your core values. Imagine what type of passion, purpose, and productivity would be ignited as a result of collaborating with shared-values-driven professionals. Imagine how many more possibilities would exist in making your vision a reality as a result of the culture you have intentionally crafted and tended to each day.

Now imagine what it would look like if that same hire was required to work with someone who repeatedly violated those values. Imagine the type of frustration, anxiety, and disconnect that would be present if that culture killer was not fired but promoted. Imagine how limited your options would be in creating trust, buy-in, and collaboration around making your vision a reality because you chose not to tend to your culture.

There's a significant difference between the two. Could you feel it as you read those words? Could you see yourself in each of those environments and envision where you might be able to shift to get in better alignment with making your company's vision a reality?

Now that we've examined many of the behaviors correlated with the soft-skill ways you can incorporate your values into your culture, let's take a look at some of the more technical or hard-skill ways you can take those steps by weaving your core values into your operations. Hard skills are learned abilities developed and strengthened through practice, repetition, and education. One might consider a certain level of certification, credential, or training in a hard skill. They are known to increase employee productivity and efficiency and to subsequently improve employee satisfaction. It all comes down to this: You value what you invest in. And when you value your values (ha!), then you damn well better back that up with your money, time, systems, and resources.

Let's say that you have the value of growth, but you don't invest in further growth opportunities with your team. Apparently, there's no money for trainings, conferences, or even certifications. No time for coaching, feedback, or reviews. No system through which employees can understand where they're going in their career growth and what exists for them in the future. No resources for people to explore what's possible for their own evolution in their roles.

Tell me, does that sound like a company that knows, owns, and lives the value of growth?

Hell-to-the-no they don't! So why proclaim it if you can't back it up in actions, policies, procedures, and budgets? This is when you truly know whether a company is living in full alignment with their core values.

These methods were illuminating when I applied them to my own business. I might be a values expert, but I had missed several internal processes that were resulting in ongoing misalignment. I spoke about inner harmony but kept taking on people and projects that consistently created chaos. I was working from a fear-based mindset instead of one grounded in our values when push came to shove. And now that I have clearly defined expectations and procedures around how things are prioritized, invested in, and chosen, we've more than doubled our revenue during a global pandemic and have never felt more in sync with our purpose; we're living our values every single day.

Here are some key ways in which you can sync your values with your daily operations and get your organization on the path to living your values more authentically.

Hiring and Onboarding

At a big annual conference I attended, the keynote speaker gave a moving talk on how their company lives their core values. She went on and on, making grand statements about the ways in which they harnessed their beliefs to create a powerful culture of engagement, retention, and profit. My heart was alive as I heard her speak; I felt like, "Yes! This is music to my ears!" When they opened it up to questions from the audience, I ran to the microphone and asked her how they vet their candidates for new positions in relation to their core values.

In an instant, I lost my warm fuzzies as she fumbled through her words, made grandiose statements with no grounding, and wasn't able to give one clear example of how they did that. In that moment, I knew that although they may have some stories to tell about their culture, they were not truly integrating their values into their operations.

What happens when a team goes through this whole process and then a new position opens up and it's time to bring a new team member on board? They haven't gone through the real-time buy-in of knowing, owning, and living the values, so how can they be expected to have that understanding of their importance in the culture and the expectations of their own behavior each day?

A CEO I collaborate with shared with me that every Wednesday he and his wife lead a Soul Circle with all their team members. It's a time for each person to share updates on what's been on their minds, hearts, and spirits and how the team might be able to support them. When I heard about that, a shot of love went up my spine. Everything about it rang true to my values, and I was so excited to learn that he was creating such a sacred experience in his culture. But what if someone was hired onto his team and wasn't told about Soul Circle Wednesdays? And what if vulnerability and authenticity did not resonate with that person? That talking about their personal lives at work was nauseating to them and felt like a waste of time? It would be unfortunate for that new hire, and it would be unfortunate for the person who wasn't hired who would have found that to be a transformative experience.

It's straight-up unfair, unkind, and inconsiderate *not* to vet new employees for values fit. How can they authentically uphold your value promises if the values don't resonate with them in the first place? You are setting them and the company up for disconnect if you don't. But when you do, you're setting them up for a true connection and sense of belonging. At the end of the day, you want your team members to know the difference between simply working somewhere and *belonging* somewhere. You and your team members can organically feel the gifts of belonging by connecting through and with your shared company values.

Let's look at the ways you can do that on purpose.

- **Include your values in job descriptions.** Make sure that people applying to the role understand up front what matters to you. This will help to attract applicants who feel a connection to them in their own search process. HR executive Christina Moniodis shared with me that at her company, "The responsibilities noted within a job description should be listed according to their importance and the frequency with which they are performed. The first bullet in each of our job descriptions, no matter the position, speaks to the expectations related to our core values. I find this so meaningful as it confirms the passion surrounding our values and how truly important they are in each and every role."

- **Ask values-aligned interview questions.** One of the most obvious but often overlooked ways to assure values alignment between your organization and candidates is to incorporate core values into the interview process. Many times people believe that it's enough to simply share their values and ask others what they think of them. What candidate is going to say that they don't agree with your values? Well, perhaps some (either the most aligned or the most unaligned), but most are looking to make a good impression. Instead of teeing up the values with a presentation, what if you went through a mini-version of your values work with them? Ask them what each value means to them and how it shows up in their lives. You could even ask for candidates to share stories of when they had to harness that value in the workplace. Try this framework, subbing in your own values where relevant:

- Our values here are reflection, connection, and growth. I'd love to know what those mean to you personally.

- Putting our company aside for the moment, how would you define these values in your own life?

- Where have they worked for you?

- When have you had stumbling blocks with them?

- Tell me a story about a time in your life where one of these values drove you. What were the circumstances, and what was the outcome?

The more you can use values as an opening conversation to get to understand the lens of the prospective new team member, the better. There isn't a right or wrong response, but you'll get a good idea of whether the person authentically connects with those concepts or whether they're forcing the answer. And by the final round of interviews, it's a proven practice to share the expectations around your value promises in greater depth. Be sure that they know what's expected of them if they come on board so that it's not a shocker after they accept the role. This is often a really rewarding and unexpected experience for soon-to-be hires, realizing that this place takes their culture seriously.

We did this recently with a new hire, and she told me later how much it made her feel like a part of the team from the start. She could tell how much we cared about the culture we'd been crafting and appreciated the time we took to set clear expectations before she accepted the offer. It was rewarding to hear that unsolicited feedback weeks after she was onboarded. And you can get that same response!

- **Ask values-aligned reference questions.** The process of checking references is also a key moment in which to learn whether the candidate's perspective on how they relate to the company's values aligns with the reference's experience. Here you could use a similar style as you did when speaking with the candidate, but instead of asking the reference what the values mean to them, recap what they mean to your organization and ask them to provide an example of when the candidate embodied that value. You can decide if you want to do it with all the values or just have them pick from this list. However, if you really want to get meaningful feedback on someone, I'd recommend that you walk through the values one at a time.

It might sound something like this: "Our company's culture is driven by our values of reflection, connection, and growth. For us, reflection is about taking the time to pause, slow down, and celebrate what's gone well and evolve where we have opportunity to do better. Connection is about how important the bonds are between our team members and with our clients. Growth comes down to recognizing that there are always opportunities to get stronger. When it comes to Kait's candidacy in this role, would you please share a story on how she's lived the values of reflection, connection, and/or growth?"

- **Review the interview process and experience.** If you claim to have the value of integrity or accountability and then you don't follow up or follow through with prospective candidates, are you really living your value? If you say that you have the value of kindness or gratitude, are you being kind and appreciative of the effort, work, and vulnerability that goes into the experience of interviewing for a job?

Take the time to put yourself in the shoes of a prospective employee, and go on the journey to learn where you can be more in alignment with your values. If you really want to know how you're doing, ask people who just went through the process, even folks who didn't get offered the job. A simple Interview Experience Survey can make a world of difference in understanding where you can be in better alignment. A survey question might sound like this:

> Opening: We care deeply about our culture, and the hiring process is a significant part of that. Please let us know how you experienced our values during your interview process.
>
> Question 1: On a scale of 1 to 10, how well did you experience our value of transparency?
>
> Question 2: Please let us know why you made the above selection.

You can repeat that pattern for every one of your values. It's staggering how much you can learn from people when you ask them direct and meaningful questions instead of engaging in the standard box-checking experience.

- **Incorporate onboarding.** You must teach the values to live the values. As I've said, by the time your new hire makes it to the onboarding stage, they should already be familiar with your values. It would be unfair to hire someone if they weren't. Now that they're being trained on what it means to work in your organization, it's crucial that the values make their way into that process in an even bigger way. Consider doing a mini-workshop or facilitated exercise where new hires get a chance to connect with other newbies to hear how they experience your values in their own lives and what their intentions are of how they can live them while at work. The more you can guide people to internalize and understand the values with their own lens, the more likely they are to remember and adopt them in their daily practices.

Onboarding is also a great time to let people know the recognition opportunities and review processes that are directly connected to these core beliefs. You might even bring in a guest speaker (either internal or external) who can talk about how they experience the values of your organization and what type of difference it's made in their relationship to the work.

There's a great quote by Benjamin Franklin that fits perfectly here: "Tell me and I forget, teach me and I may remember, involve me and I learn."

- **Give permission to be human.** Every one of us is in a different stage of our journey. Knowing if a candidate can relate to, name, and embrace values isn't the sole determinant of whether a person will be a great team member. Recognize that most people have anxiety during major changes and opportunities in life, and assume the best about them if they didn't give you the perfect answer. If you're on the fence, give them another chance to express and share themselves. Conscious business leaders know that listening to your intuition about someone's character and skills is just as important as listening to the answers a candidate is sharing with you.

Budgets and Investments

Because I'm not a finance expert or an accountant, I reached out to my accountant, Matt Bralove, and former consulting CFO Kesha-Simone Jones to weigh in and share their genius. It was fascinating to hear how different yet similar their perspectives were to my own. They shared that in their consulting businesses, they repeatedly saw that it was easy to say that you had values until money was involved—which goes both ways. You need money to invest in the things that reflect your values and you also need money to have a sustainable business so that you're not operating out of lack, scarcity, and fear when making decisions. It's very hard to do that when there is no profit.

Getting clear on the company's money blocks, flows, and opportunities, in good times and bad, sets the stage for leaders to make more intentional choices about their budgets and investments.

During the pandemic, many organizations were butting up against this experience. Business as usual was no more. Entire industries shut down. Companies were struggling to figure out how to stay afloat. I know of a company that, prior to the pandemic, actively honored their value of family first. Whenever there was a question of whether an employee should clock more billable hours or spend time with their family, the company always prioritized family. They knew that if their people were with their families, they would be happier and better employees. When COVID hit, their employees fully embraced family first, but the company's profits suffered, and their clients suffered. It was a true conundrum for them.

One partner was always waving the family-first flag while the other was waving the profit-first flag. They admitted that when things got tough, values didn't matter—cash mattered. Cash is king is the mindset of the majority of business leaders. What leaders don't easily realize is that the more deeply grounded they are in their values, the more clearly and readily they can make choices for the business budgets and investments that carry them through the uncertainty and ultimately cement them into more solid financial ground.

Where we invest is a direct reflection of what we value. If we value our values, we'll double down on ensuring that they have the money required to back them up and give them the foundation they need to exist and not starve.

- **Share budget basics.** Your budget needs to be a tool for you to execute your vision, mission, and values. There's no real risk in a budget, as it can change at any time. So instead of simply throwing out numbers, create definitions of what those numbers mean and how you want them to make you feel. How much money will it take to create that feeling? Most business owners struggle to get to a big number. When they do, it creates a new thirst that makes that number never big enough. Unless your company's core value is wealth, chasing the number will pull you away from your values.

There's a company I work with that has doubled their business revenue every year, but the owner isn't happy. He has an internal tug-of-war because he knows they're not investing that money into things that will allow them to truly embrace their value of balance. If they invested in the tools and technology that would alleviate their extensive time sucks, then it might be possible. But the company is moving so fast, so quickly that they haven't taken the time to pause, see what they're investing in, and make choices that enable their team to work smarter instead of harder.

- **Define success.** Define success by asking yourself the following questions:

  - What kind of organization are we really trying to build?

  - How do we define success?

  - How does our success align with our values?

  - Is it based on a certain dollar amount?

  - How much does that dollar amount have to change each year?

  - How are we going to define success for this season?

  - What do we really want?

  - How can we build a budget and a profit based on that picture, not based on what others think or what we see other organizations doing?

- **Identify values-aligned allocations.** When determining your budget, are your allocations a true reflection of your values? If you have the value of excellence, is there a significant budget allocated for your team members to have the equipment they need to deliver excellent services? If you have the value of inclusion, is there money put aside for proper training to illuminate unconscious bias within your team? If you have the value of community, does your leadership invest in paying for experiences that build a sense of connection? It's one thing to say that you care about something in your words; it's an entirely different thing to back it up in your investments. When I look at someone's budget, I can tell you very quickly what a company values in reality and compare it to their stated core values. It's one of these obvious disconnects that somehow keeps going under the radar.

On the flip side, I've known companies that have massively invested in their values-driven culture—so much so that profit didn't matter to them in the moment. It was truly about what was right for their people. And guess what? The return they got on that investment was always more significant than the dollars down:

- Eighty percent of employees felt more engaged when their work was consistent with the core values and mission of their organization (IBM).[45]

- Ninety-three percent of workers at companies with recognition programs tied to core values agree that the work they do has meaning and purpose (Globoforce).[46]

---

45 IBM Smarter Workforce Institute, "The Employee Experience Index," IBM, July 2017, https://www.ibm.com/downloads/cas/JDMXPMBM.

46 WorkHuman Research Institute, "Bringing More Humanity to Recognition, Performance, and Life at Work," Globoforce, 2017, https://www.globoforce.com/wp-content/uploads/2017/10/WHRI_2017SurveyReportA.pdf.

- Seventy-seven percent of employees agree that a strong culture allows them to do their best work, 76 percent see the impact in productivity and efficiency, and 74 percent draw a correlation between culture and their ability to serve their customer base (Eagle Hill Consulting).[47]

- **Try it before you buy it.** You can't simply invest money into your values as a way to solve or get ahead of the problem. When you make these financial investments, you must also be willing to invest in your own hours, people, and resources. Otherwise you could have a case of throwing money at something that doesn't get used or adopted into your cultural norms.

For example, I had a team member who was manually transcribing interviews daily. He told me how difficult it was and how much energy it was taking out of him. Thinking that I was being helpful and activating our value of inner harmony, I invested in a top-rated piece of equipment to help with transcription. I didn't take any time to learn how to use it or to see if it was even worthwhile for us to implement. I just gave it to him and expected it to solve his problems. It didn't. I essentially flushed that money down the toilet because I did not take the time to truly understand the issue and get involved in a solution that was bigger than just transcription. It was connected to workload and expectations.

You might think, "Well, I'm giving my money. Therefore, I budgeted for this tool to support inner harmony and balance. That's enough." If you do not invest in the conversation but are willing to write a check, you're only halfway there. Next time you're ready to invest money into a solution, ask yourself, "Am I

47 Eagle Hill Consulting, "The Business Case for Culture."

paying for this to try to make a problem go away?" or "Am I paying for this because I've gotten curious about the problem and know this solution will get us further ahead?" Be willing to slow down in order to get ahead.

- **Be transparent.** This may seem extreme for some, but it's a proven practice that both my accountant and CFO heavily subscribe to. Share your numbers with your people whenever possible. We often think that this will be too much for people to take in, but it ultimately creates more ownership and understanding of the overall business structure. If you're not comfortable with showing it all, share percentages and connect those percentages to your values. Total them up and present that to your people. It could be as simple as family first: 50 percent; freedom: 30 percent; community: 20 percent.

- **Practice what you preach.** So many companies talk out of both sides of their mouths. They preach about how much they care about their values but then their practices are totally disconnected. This is significant when it comes to budgets and investments. For example, a company might say that they have the value of well-being, but even while knowing how stretched the team already is, they keep making executive decisions to lay off team members and expect the folks still employed to carry all their leftover workload in order to make a bigger profit. Or perhaps a company expects everyone to live their values but they don't invest in any support to help coach, train, or engage team members in their personal growth relative to these values. It's mostly common sense that isn't so common.

When teams do practice what they preach, true alignment exists.

I had the privilege of working alongside Dr. Charles Johnson-Bey when he was leading the Cyber Innovations team at Lockheed Martin. This man is a genius when it comes to math, science, and humanity. When he took over his newly formed team, he reached out. Charles was effective at connecting one-on-one but wanted his team members to feel a greater connection to each other. His goal was for the team to have solid bonds that inspired ongoing collaboration.

After I facilitated a successful series of values-based workshops and trainings, he had a vision for the ultimate experience together: a retreat at Disney World. Charles invited his team to join him at their Orlando location for strategic planning, connection, collaboration, and fun. My role was to embody those values during our time at the theme park and facilitate more focused values work over dinner. It was the definition of magic—exciting, unexpected, and inspiring.

From the time we boarded the plane to the time we sat down for dinner, organic (yet intentional) sparks were flying. After only a few hours of waiting in lines and experiencing the latest attractions together, a new level of trust and connection was reached. Our drive back from the park to the hotel included full-volume carpool karaoke and storytelling about our passions outside of work; deep new bonds cemented between us.

How did that happen? It wasn't "just because" we were at Disney World—that's not a silver bullet solution. It happened because every single person chose to invest in being there—physically, emotionally, and financially. They chose to let go of normal workplace formalities, embrace the magic, and ignite new possibilities to truly know each other. This investment sent a massive message to the team that their leader wants them to collaborate more often and have fun while doing it.

- **Remember that cheaper isn't always better.** I'm all about saving money. I was raised in a home whose motto was ACAP (as cheap as possible) when it came to our purchases. But as I grew older, I learned firsthand that you get what you pay for. If communication is a core value and you invest only in the cheapest online course you can find to help train people in their public speaking skills, you will likely get the results that you paid for. That's not to say that there aren't incredible affordable options these days, but it's worth looking beyond the price tag to determine whether the product will support your people and truly set them up for success.

- **Give permission to be human.** Although your accounting and finance team needs to be top notch at these financial factors, not all team members are numbers people and will have an easy time with their budgets. Tune in to which leaders may need some more support, and determine who can coach, mentor, or train them to sharpen those skills—or even have them collaborate with someone who is already a pro to ensure that people are working in their genius. I heard a soccer coach once say, "I would never ask my goalie to practice scoring goals. They need to be the best at stopping them. Why would we waste our time building skills that they don't really need when it counts?"

Reviews and Rewards

Some people love them, and others loathe them: annual reviews. For starters, let's just get it out in the open that waiting an entire year to give someone one review is never a good idea—even if that person is crushing their goals. The ongoing opportunity to check in, give guidance, and celebrate wins and then reward people for them creates psychological safety, belonging, and purpose.

The cadence and pace of that process needs to reflect your values and cultural norms. I'm not saying, "The review must be monthly for forty-five minutes at a time with this specific agenda." Although monthly reviews might be right for your company, bi-monthly or even quarterly ones might be better for another. Or perhaps it's a quarterly retreat where you have one-on-one time with each person while also team building with the larger group. You get to choose.

The key is to make sure that reviews are done with metrics and a frequency where your people won't be completely surprised if they're totally on the mark or not even close. Make sure that new team members are just as aware as tenured ones of what to expect. It's never too early to get clear on your expectations between managers, team members, and the review process so that there's full agreement among all involved. Remember: Expectations – Agreement = Disappointment.

Get ahead of that and you'll have a team that looks forward to these opportunities and feels a true sense of accomplishment when they're rewarded for reaching and exceeding expectations. When rewards like annual bonuses are tied to performance, team members have an opportunity to be seen, recognized, and valued in a way that's directly connected to their efforts and behavior.

- **Deliver ongoing reviews.** Sitting someone down one time a year to review performance is a robotic way of doing business. I recommend that during ongoing one-on-ones, there is at least one conversation per month dedicated to how the team member is doing with their values alignment. This is not something that you want to let go on for months and months without addressing, so why wait for a formal process to have these important conversations? Make it normal and routine—an expectation that your organization and its team members will be held accountable.

- **Practice values-based metrics.** In the review itself, it's a proven practice to include metrics around each value so that there is a fair and equitable process on the side of the manager giving the review and the employee receiving it. You can use a scale in which there's a rubric for scoring whether that person is living the company's value promises.

It could look like this:

Metrics: Based on frequency of keeping the value promise through behaviors.

3	2	1	0
Often	Sometimes	Seldom	Never

Value: Curiosity

Value Promise 1: When faced with frustration, we promise to ask thoughtful questions with the intention to gain a better understanding of the matter at hand.
Score: 3

Feedback: *I appreciate how much more you've been asking questions since it came up in our last one-on-one. I hope it's been helpful in reducing your stress. Keep it up, and let me know how I can continue to support you.*

Value Promise 2: We promise to speak up and follow our curiosity in order to ignite more innovation and personal growth.
Score: 1

Feedback: *I am glad you're asking more questions and encourage you to take that same momentum to speak up more without being prompted. I know there's a lot of great stuff brewing inside you, and it would benefit us all if we heard more of it. Let me know if another format of communication may be a better starting point. We'll figure this out!*

Value Promise 3: We promise to connect more deeply with ourselves and our team members by asking quality questions and consciously listening.
Score: 2

Feedback: *I know how much closer your team has gotten since you went on your retreat recently. Thanks for making the space to be fully present. I'd love to see you continue to make time for that type of connection throughout the week.*

Total Points: 6/9

Consider involving both clients and team members in this review too. It doesn't have to be just one person's perspective of that colleague. It's best to get perspective from a variety of angles.

- **Provide opportunities to realign.** If you have a thoughtful review process like the one just outlined, there's a real chance for team members to get back in alignment with the company's core values when they've gotten off their intended path. This is where vulnerability, empathy, and empowerment play a significant role. It's hard to tell someone that they're not meeting expectations, and it's hard to be on the receiving end of hearing that statement. This is where your one-on-one coaching techniques from chapter 7 really come into play. Be thoughtful in your approach and delivery, and there will be a much more connecting experience instead of one that leaves people feeling sad, annoyed, pissed off, or wrongfully judged.

- **Offer values-aligned bonuses and promotions.** Once you go through these review processes, make sure that the promotions and bonuses sync up with that individual's embodiment of the core values. When a consistent values violator is promoted, people immediately lose trust in the higher-up's judgment, and they also start to lose interest in being held accountable to the stated values.

How can you hold someone else accountable to something that you're not doing yourself? OK, so you can do that, but trust me—people don't respect it, and they will gossip about it. When you do hold yourself to the same standards as those you're overseeing, it ignites inspiration, trust, and respect for the process. Next time you determine your bonuses and promotions, be sure that it's through an equitable lens that truly honors the culture you intend to build.

- **Give permission to be human.** Whether someone is a
  top performer or not, the review process can be anxiety-
  inducing for many people. The fear of judgment, criticism,
  and not-enoughness naturally bubbles up when we're walking into a situation in which we're there to be critiqued
  and potentially paid accordingly. I can remember a time
  when I was working my butt off, getting loads of positive
  feedback and accolades all year long, yet when the time
  came for annual reviews, I didn't get a promotion that I
  had assumed was a given. It was painful and made me
  completely rethink why I was giving my all to an organization that didn't value it. Recognize that other humans will
  feel this way, too, and be thoughtful in your approach to
  sharing your feedback.

Policies and Procedures

In your company's employee handbook, you likely have a whole
bunch of policies and procedures listed. Some people will read it
and refer to it regularly. Others will never open it outside of the
required signatures for HR. Either way, it's still important that
your values have a home there.

Here are some ideas on where to start.

- **Highlight your values.** This is the most obvious, but again,
  it's something that's often overlooked. In the section of
  your handbook or employee manual that cites your vision,
  mission, and values, include how the values were formed,
  how they're upheld, and the value promises that underline
  the specific expectation so that each team member can
  embody them every day. Make it clear that these are more
  than just nice ideas and marketing collateral.

- **Use plain, jargon-free language.** As someone who came from the nonprofit sector before starting my business, I am quite familiar with jargon. We do-gooders often rely on it to get a point across, but it doesn't always serve us or the person reading it. Do your best to use plain, easy-to-follow language so that people can get it right away and don't have to decode it or hire a lawyer to understand its meaning.

- **Use small, scannable chunks.** When policies and procedures look like legal documents, it's highly unlikely that people will be able to understand them. It takes a certain type of learner who can easily process that form of information. Wherever you can, break sections up and use images, lists, charts, or icons. Get to the point of what you have to say so that it doesn't take a rocket scientist to decipher what you're intending to share.

- **Give permission to be human.** Most people won't treat their employee manual as bedside table reading. Let's be honest. When new employees come aboard, a lot is going on, and it's likely that although they may need to sign pages of the manual and review them with you in real time, they will need to be examined again and again if you want them to stick. Don't make the mistake of thinking that information is now locked into someone's thinking or way of being. Most humans need to hear something at least seven times before it sticks. So if it really matters, make sure that there are opportunities to engage and digest the information outside of the traditional policy and procedure conversations.

Systems and Processes

There are formal and informal systems and processes in every organization. Some make things run a lot smoother, and some create a bottleneck. These are often the areas of opportunity where people start to say things like this: "If it ain't broke, don't fix it." "That's too complicated; let's not overthink it." "That's the way we've always done it." "We tried, and that's never worked for us before." "I don't have the time to overhaul that." The reality is that if your culture really is out of alignment with your values, you haven't tried it this way and you are constantly wasting time by not pausing to look at it and make better choices for your efficiency, productivity, and well-being. If you were to sift through each of these areas in your organization, I bet you'd find some gold.

- **Set boundaries with your schedule.** The way we spend our time is a direct reflection of that phrase "actions speak louder than words." If you say that you want your people to have space to process, reflect, and grow, do your actions and schedules mirror that intention? I work with leaders all over the world and am constantly hearing about their jam-packed schedules, which often bleed into the evenings and weekends. They have a desperate desire to get a grip on their day-to-day flow but think that it comes with the territory of being a leader.

We often give our power over to what other people want from us instead of setting boundaries that help us ensure that we're not constantly in a state of feeling overwhelmed.

As I've said before, the best thing any leader can do is to model the behavior they want to see in others. You want your team to be less stressed? Then show them what a schedule looks like for someone who isn't constantly overwhelmed and who puts a stake in the ground with their boundaries. These can be simple adjustments or more complex analysis. You get to choose.

Here are some examples of schedule policies that I've created around our value of inner harmony:

- No external meetings on Mondays and Fridays.

- No more than three external meetings a day Tuesday through Thursday (a maximum of nine meetings per week).

- Determine a quitting time every day, and don't work afterward.

I did this exercise with eight unique value statements, descriptions, and associated policies. I've blocked these out in my calendar and put reminders where I would most easily slip up. For example, on Mondays and Fridays, my schedule reads, "PROTECTED: Value Policy." I've caught myself trying to sneak in an appointment on one of those days. Then that block shows up, and because of the language I used, it stops me in my tracks. If I had written "Hold" or "Do not book," it wouldn't have carried an ounce of the power that these words do for me. It also helps that my administrative assistant knows to never offer those days up for external meetings when she's scheduling appointments.

If you wanted to take a more analytical approach, try color-coding your meetings. Start by thinking about the categories or types of meetings that you have on a regular basis and the percentage of your time that you want to dedicate to that category. Consider how that category relates to your core values. Then choose a color that represents those different types of meetings and begin to make a connection like the following:

Category	% of Time	Color Code	Value
Professional development	20%	green	growth
Staff support	35%	orange	growth
Client support	25%	blue	loyalty
Relationship development	20%	yellow	loyalty

As you can see, I also added the value that was connected to that category of meetings. Looking at this list, would it feel in alignment with your intentions to have 55 percent of your time spent on growth and 45 percent of your time spent on loyalty? You get to decide and adjust your choices in how you invest your time accordingly.

Go through your schedule with your own color-coding system and update the meeting appointment colors. Finally, see if your intended percentages are an actual reflection of the time you're spending on these items in reality.

If they're out of alignment, start to time block your days and weeks to support your process to get back in sync. Perhaps you want to block entire days or weeks to certain aspects of work? When you time block your schedule to prioritize your values and those correlated actions, your life will change and you'll give others permission to do the same.

- **Make your out-of-office response human.** I know that out-of-office messages can seem inconsequential, but every message we send (automated or handwritten) is an opportunity to ignite connection through our shared humanity. These autoresponses are created to set expectations and allow us to feel like we can step away without worry that someone may think we're ignoring them. They are useful and necessary when it comes to workflow and boundaries.

Next time you have to alert people that you'll be unavailable, consider sharing what you're up to and how it activates your values. Instead of the classic "Sorry I missed you. I'm out of the office until [DATE], with limited access to email. If you require immediate assistance, please email […]," consider your version of an authentic approach.

Mine often reads like this: "Thank you for reaching out. I'm currently on retreat in the mountains of Idaho. I will be disconnected from technology to reconnect with my humanity over the next ten days. My values of reflection, unity with nature, and growth will be in full force. I hope you're able to prioritize your values as a tool for well-being too."

- **Set realistic deadlines.** Are your deadlines serving or hurting your team? A new CEO told me that she couldn't believe what the people in her company had been doing to themselves before she took over. There were deadlines that were created for vanity metrics instead of for the capacity and ability of the team. Decades of these practices had led to the buildup and breakdown of mental health for her team members.

So many companies have massive year-end deadline processes. They ignite unnecessary levels of pressure and stress because they have come to believe that they'll all turn into a pumpkin on midnight in the new year. All kidding aside, there are some legal reasons that you may need to do certain things before year-end; however, you likely don't have to do everything at that same time.

- **Develop a values-aligned strategic plan.** So many teams go through an extensive strategic planning process every few years. And those very teams often miss the opportunity to incorporate their plans through the lens of their values. Whether you hire a consultant or make these plans internally, be sure that you start by reviewing your values and value promises so that they function as your compass and guardrails for your future plans and intentions. It can be as significant as entire initiatives based on your values, or it could simply be a callout box that highlights the values that are tied to the plans. As with the values filter questions from chapter 7, this is a perfect time to harness your values for genuine alignment as you build toward the future.

- **Know your systems.** The most common systems include payroll, personnel, accounts receivable, accounts payable, and inventory. Here are some general questions to ask yourself when looking at the effectiveness of your systems:

  - How can we reduce the steps in this process?

  - How can we combine steps to make the process simpler to follow?

  - Can we repurpose an existing system or tool to save us time or give us a better result?

  - How can we speed up this process or any step within this process?

- How can we automate this process (or any part of this process)?

- How can we semiautomate this process (or any part of this process)?

- How can we template this process (or any part of this process)?

- How can we lower the costs of completing this process without affecting the value of the output?

- What simple changes or improvements can we make to increase the value of the output?

- Who else in the world has a related process or tool that we can learn from to help us better design this process?[48]

- How can this process more effectively align with our values?

- **Review operational processes.** A business or operational process is an organized set of activities or tasks that produces a specific service or product. The process of providing a haircut, for example, often has three main parts: first hair washing, then the actual cutting, and finally styling with a brush and hair dryer. These processes are directly

---

48 David Finkel, "10 Questions to Ask When You Design or Redesign a Process," *Inc.*, January 29, 2015, https://www.inc.com/david-finkel/10-questions-to-ask-when-you-design-or-redesign-a-process.html.

tied to how you generate income. So doesn't that make them valuable?[49]

When looking at your operations through your values lens, consider if they are a true reflection or a nice idea that didn't quite land. Let's use the example of the hair salon and the values of collaboration, connection, and beauty. As you walk through the process of how someone gets their hair washed, does the customer experience collaboration, connection, and beauty? Perhaps another team member takes on this piece of the work with collaboration. Perhaps the conversation during the wash or even just asking whether the temperature is OK creates connection. Perhaps the customer is treated with such kindness and support that they feel beautiful already.

Pretty simple. But the idea of updating and tweaking your processes by going on the customer's journey will support your values and can run pretty deep. Asking your customers for feedback is an incredible way to amp up these processes too. Be direct. Ask, "How did you experience our values of connection, collaboration, and beauty? What's one thing that we could do differently to better infuse our values into your experience here?"

- **Review support processes.** Aptly named, these are any systems that support the operational processes. This could include HR, financial management, building and property management, IT, security, corporate governance, quality management, and more. Using the salon example again, you might think about the processes around how to schedule an appointment, how you pay your bills, and whether

---

49 Knowledge@Wharton High School, "Operational Process," University of Pennsylvania, February 28, 2011, https://kwhs.wharton.upenn.edu/term/operational-process/.

the building itself is clean and equipped with the tools necessary to follow through on your services with ease and grace. Using the same values lens as before, it would be a fascinating filter to ask: Do these processes reflect collaboration, connection, and beauty?

- **Review management processes.** The management process begins with the three basic elements of this work: ideas, things, and people. Management of these three elements is directly related to conceptual thinking (of which planning is an essential part), administration, and leadership.[50]

Much of this was covered in chapter 7; however, I would be remiss in not including it here, in terms of how managers go about creating and adhering to their processes. In many cases, there is not a standardized process in these areas, but they could benefit from the creation of one. Other times, there are processes that are a total waste of time and that need to come to an end, such as weekly activity reports that are never reviewed or data entry of tasks that are never tracked. How might your management processes better reflect your values?

- **Give permission to be human.** Like culture, one system or process will not fit all. Recognize the nuances of leadership and learning styles, and try not to be too rigid. There is always opportunity to improve, so invite those possibilities in. It's worth saying again: Avoid using phrases like "We've always done it that way" or "If it ain't broke, don't

---

50 R. Alec Mackenzie, "The Management Process in 3D," *Harvard Business Review*, republished online from November 1969, https://hbr.org/1969/11/the-management-process-in-3-d.

fix it." These sayings shut down potential for innovation, connection, and a better way of solving problems.

Terminations and Exit Interviews

The way your company hires and fires people is a true reflection of your culture. There are places that have no issue letting people go at the drop of a hat to cut costs, and there are places that do everything they can to coach and support people before they gracefully direct them to another organization that may be a better fit for their skills. Those are the two ends of the spectrum, and there's a ton in between.

Whenever possible, you want to ensure that the way you terminate a person is a reflection of your values and that you take the time to get legitimate feedback through their unique lens before they're gone.

I was once in an exit interview in which the HR manager kept asking me if I would take her with me. Every time she asked a question off her list, she started to vent about her own issues with the organization. *It was nuts!* And at the same time, it was a straight-up reflection of the culture, which was infested with gossip, and that's exactly what I had experienced. Precisely for that reason, I didn't give the full feedback that I had inside me because it felt unsafe to do so. Instead, I asked the head of HR to lunch with me weeks afterward, and she graciously accepted. I ultimately learned that my feedback made no difference after I shared it. But it was what I needed to do to feel whole in my transition.

Can you imagine how quickly and precisely you could shift your culture if, when people left, they spoke the truth about what happened—and then the organization did something with it? I wish that were the norm, but shockingly, it's far from it. Especially if you're losing a culture keeper, this is a key moment to get insight into how you can create a culture that's in better alignment with your values.

There are obviously times when you need to get someone out of their role and out of the company with urgency. In those cases, it's more important to protect the well-being of your current employees than to do your best to ensure that you support their transition plans. I've worked with companies where people were downright emotionally, mentally, and verbally abusive to their team members, and they needed to be ushered out of the office by security. That was the best option. But, hopefully, you're doing your greatest to create a culture where it never gets to that extreme, where people are picking up on the signs that something is off and it's discussed and mediated before an explosion of mass scale occurs.

This is yet another opportunity to exercise empathy with boundaries. This concept is one that rocked my world when I learned it from Brené Brown because I was sure that boundaries were separate from empathy. When we let people do things that are not OK with us, they are crossing our boundaries whether they (or we) realize it or not. We cannot *feel with someone* (empathy) if they are breaking our boundaries. If and when you get to a place where someone needs to move on from your company, boundaries must be in place first. What's OK and what's not OK? Make those expectations clear. From there you can lead with empathy for their circumstances and take grounded, conscious action. Try these concepts out to get your process even more solidified as a reflection of your values.

- **Avoid surprises.** I get that these are ideal situations, not what necessarily happens in real life. Having said that, I recommend that you do your best to be sure that a termination is not coming out of nowhere. Whether the decision is due to downsizing or a behavioral issue, make people aware of the possibility before they are told that they are no longer employed with you. When appropriate, put someone on a performance improvement plan and provide coaching to give them a chance at changing. At the same time, it's never a good idea to let culture killers run rampant. You must be willing to terminate someone who violates your core values, and they should be made aware of the relevant incidents as soon as possible.

- **Take action in person, in private.** In the remote-work world we live in now, you may not be able to take these actions in person. At least create a virtual video connection so that you are face-to-face with the person being terminated. It can feel inhumane to be terminated within a public setting and for you not to have the decency to look someone in the eye when you do it.

I came across the book *Mastering Civility,* by Christine Porath, while I felt like I was trapped in a company that treated people uncivilly. As a business school professor, she offers original and humane insight about dealing with interpersonal workplace issues. When I was looking for guidance, answers, or data that would help me be more effective in my role, her book was eye-opening. In chapter after chapter, I gained more and more insights about what was commonplace and what I could do about it. I remembered when she shared a story about a team that was fired over email:

> How would you feel if you received the following email: The workforce reduction notification is currently in progress. Unfortunately your position is one that has been eliminated. That's how four

hundred RadioShack employees found out that they had lost their job. Wholly uncivil. But, sadly not as rare as it should be. All too often we turn instinctively to email when we're dealing with difficult situations that need to be addressed face-to-face, or at least over the phone. The number one act for which people fault themselves in the civility quiz is using email when face-to-face communication is needed. Sensitive issues, conflict situations, and performance reviews all call for an actual, physical presence. A good rule of thumb: If you're wondering whether you should send that email, stop. Don't send it. Pick up the phone or meet face-to-face.[51]

- **Provide honest feedback.** If someone is being terminated as a result of unmet expectations, it's helpful to provide them with meaningful feedback. You must use your discretion to determine whether that person is open to receiving your feedback, but it's a gift to provide the feedback if it's done with empathy and care for their future. This might be the only time this person can get honest tips, tools, and coaching on how they might be more successful in their next endeavor or what types of roles might be a better fit for their skills and interests.

- **Ask values-aligned exit interview questions.** Just like the hiring process, this is another key time to ask people about how they experienced the company's values while they were employed with you. This can be through a formal survey and/or an open conversation. Employees on their

---

51 Porath, 113.

way out are likely to speak more openly about their experiences. But again, without psychological safety, they will not. Consider any of these questions for your exit interview tool kit:

- Where are we most successful with living our values?

- Where do we have the greatest opportunity for growth in living our values?

- If you had a magic wand (no restrictions on your desire), what's one thing you'd change about our culture immediately?

- What was your high point in this role?

- What was your low point?

- How might we be more effective in creating a culture the reflects our core values?

- **Be supportive of their next steps.** When someone is leaving on good (or even relatively good) terms, it makes a big difference for them to be supported as a potential reference or referral for your company. Although it may be difficult to see a good person leave, imagine what might be possible if they leave in such great standing that they wind up referring you new business, being an advocate for your services, or even coming back one day when they realize how much they truly loved working with you. Trust me, you want people raving about their time working with you, not venting about how awful it was when they quit.

I once had a client whose boss threw a stapler at her and ripped her resignation letter in half when she resigned. She was a top performer, and the boss was not expecting her to take another offer because they had such a close relationship. You better believe that after that stapler went through the air (and thankfully missed her), she immediately knew that she had made the right decision and had a big story to share with people when they asked about her time there.

- **Host a transition/farewell celebration.** Whether they're leaving the organization completely or transitioning to another team within your company, consider how you might honor and celebrate this person within your team. A special lunch, a card, or even a small gathering is a great way to support people in processing their grief and having some closure around the transition. Keep in mind that the team members of the person leaving will also be going through their own grief cycles (as discussed in chapter 7).

To make this a meaningful gathering, instead of an obligatory event, consider storytelling as its heart. Invite people to go around in a circle and share their favorite memory with that person, perhaps even stories of how they lived out the core values. When it's complete, invite the person who is leaving to say a few words.

This format, when facilitated authentically, is tried and true for our human experience. We crave closure and the opportunity to make peace with change. Recognize that it's not only nice for the person leaving but also for everyone who was impacted by that person's presence.

- **Give permission to be human.** Especially if they were not expecting the termination, a person will likely go through the stages of grief amid this process. Be prepared to support someone through that journey, even if it's with a resource guide with the number of a hotline that is better suited to give that guidance. Getting your organization's operations, systems, strategies, and financials in alignment with your values is a worthy and meaningful task that is likely easier than you think. My hope is that you will start with one of these categories and intentionally work your way through them, taking into account your own values lens. These might not all make sense for your organization right now, and that's OK. Meet yourself where you are, and create a plan of action for when you'll spend time to comb through these categories and make internal changes. Using the model of a strategic plan, perhaps you want to solely focus on a values alignment strategic plan?

> If you need support, that's precisely why we created our online courses and live coaching sessions to guide you through these steps with ease and grace.

You get to decide what makes the most sense for you and your team. But please, whatever you decide, follow through! There's nothing worse than getting your people excited about meaningful change and then having them lose faith because leadership wasn't really in it for the long run. This is the kind of work that you're going to wish you had done sooner. Kind of like how I wish I'd started meditating at a younger age. My life is simply and completely better now that it's a part of my daily practice and norms. And that's what a values-aligned culture does. It creates simplicity, habits, and routines that serve you instead of holding you back from the joy of a thriving business.

Even in "technical" aspects of your business such as budgeting, performance reviews, and onboarding and termination processes, you have myriad chances to structurally incorporate your core values. Do the systems and processes that define the operation of your organization—from interviews to scheduling to employee handbook drafting—enforce your value promises at every step? Or do they feel static and isolated from your values work? The actualization of values is not only about the soft skills that constitute culture but also about the nitty-gritty of strategies and operations, the daily procedures that add up. Now that you understand how your organization can take responsibility for owning and living the values within its culture each day, let's look at how every member of your organization can embrace the role of culture keeper.

Values Alignment Review

1. It's straight-up unfair, unkind, and inconsiderate *not* to vet new employees for values fit.

2. You must teach the values to live the values.

3. Our investments are a direct reflection of what we value.

4. Waiting an entire year to give someone one review is never a good idea.

5. When a values violator gets promoted, people immediately lose trust in the higher-up's judgment and also start to lose interest in being held accountable to the values.

This chapter highlighted our Permission to Be Human Online Course.

If this opportunity sparked your interest, learn more at www. permissiontobehuman.co, or check out the SparkVision Resources section of this book.

CHAPTER 9

Building Conscious Culture Keepers through Mindfulness

Happiness is a genuine and ongoing feeling of joy and peace of mind,
the result of living congruently with one's values.
—Bob Burg

When you're leading an organization, it can feel like the weight of the world is on your shoulders. As an entrepreneur myself, I've felt the pain of not knowing whether I could afford payroll, making gut-wrenching choices on whether to fire a top paying client who is not truly a good values fit, or questioning whether I've made the right choices for my business and heart to thrive. It's because I've gone through those experiences that I also know the relief and flow that are ignited when you no longer fear things that are outside your control. There is an ease of knowing how to make difficult choices with grace by grounding yourself in your values and choosing what's truly in alignment with them instead of what's popular. And what's even better? Having a whole team that knows how to do the same.

As the African proverb says, "If you want to go fast, go alone. If you want to go far, go together." Whether you're a team of 3 or 3,333, having support in your company's journey to alignment is key. In the case of many of the companies we work with, a significant part of our efforts come into play when designing and launching a culture keepers program. As a reminder, culture keepers are the individuals who lead and maintain the positive aspects of their organization's environment, an embodiment of the company's core values. Therefore, a culture keeper program's goal is to ignite more values alignment among behaviors, actions, policies, and procedures. These are active working groups made up of advisers and implementers. They intentionally keep the pulse of your organization's culture and support strategic efforts to ensure its ongoing well-being.

Often all the "issues" and "problems" fall on managers and leadership to solve. But the reality is that you don't have to be in leadership to have a really solid answer and support system to offer up. Creating a well-oiled culture keeper program lifts the weight of solving internal staff issues off one person and creates a shared sense of responsibility for the overall health of your organization. There's no need to take it all on alone. When you have a whole team of folks supporting the day-to-day practice of living the company's core values, your culture is sure to soar.

Culture Keeper Program Structure

There are loads of ways you can design and execute your culture keeper program, and I have some key strategies and proven practices that will get you further in whatever model you choose to build. This tried-and-true structure can be the way you develop any program (beyond culture keepers) in the future.

Who to Start With

You can't lead a values-driven culture if you don't live a values-driven life. With that in mind, I highly recommend that your team for this program comprise existing culture keepers. It's best if members can speak from their own experience with proven practices, not cool ideas they've heard about somewhere but have never implemented before. It's more effective and efficient to start with what you know has worked before within a subculture of the company so that it can spread organically to more teams.

Instead of hand selecting your personal favorites, make it a democratic process by collecting a culture keeper nomination list by sending out a survey asking team members to submit the full names of staff who embody your company's values. If you already conducted a Values Alignment Survey, this is the bonus question, so you would not need to send it out separately. If you did not include it before, it can be as simple as this: "Which staff member(s) positively live the value of X? Please list their full name(s) below." Then replicate this question for each of your values. Once you've received your results, see who rises to the top with the most nominations for each value. Then use your values filter for diversity, equity, and inclusion by getting a true representation of your company. Include considerations like tenure, title, department, gender, ethnicity, generation, and location (if your organization has multiple offices). It's key to have a genuine reflection of your organization's makeup to provide diverse perspectives rather than populate the program with the usual suspects who sign up for every committee.

Keep in mind that team members can rotate so that each person eventually has a chance to serve in an advisory position. However, when you start, make sure that you're building the foundation with the *humans who are giving themselves and others permission to be human.* When you engage culture killers in designing and executing values alignment efforts, it can be detrimental to both the optics of the group and the sincerity of its reception.

What to Call It

Based on the organization's stage of values alignment and its branding taste, we've called these teams different things: Culture Builders Committee, Culture Keepers Team, Values Alignment Council, Values Champions, or Values Alignment Work Group. These teams are meant to be small enough in size to allow for all voices to be heard actively but big enough to be a true representation of the organization at large. They can meet for whatever length of time and at whatever frequency that makes sense for their culture; however, I recommend that they meet at least twice a month. Culture changes every day, after all.

How It Works

This team essentially follows a train-the-trainer model in which your culture keepers start by embodying the behaviors that you desire in others. After they've mastered each skill, they then become the trainers by piloting new practices within their teams. Once they've learned what worked and what didn't, they can share the results with one another and develop a well-tested and thought-through, proven practice model that can then be launched throughout the entire company.

Think of it this way: Do you need support in having more effective meetings, better one-on-ones, or embodiment of a specific value? Which one of your culture keepers is a wiz at that? Empower those people and lift them up to share their proven practices with everyone else. Then have each member of the program integrate those practices within their own team, starting with themselves. They can modify it to their personality and leadership style and stay consistent in the overarching concepts and behavior that you're looking to shift. Try out the new practices for an agreed-upon length of time (I recommend at least three months), and then have each culture keeper report back on their experience. What worked, what didn't, what was modified, and what was kept the same? Once those pilots are complete and you feel that you have both qualitative and quantitative data to pull together a proven practice tool kit, it's time to roll out those initiatives to the organization at large. This is an organic and thoughtful approach to human-centered design within your culture.

It's key to also note that there will be times when your culture keepers don't have proven practices to share. When they don't have the expertise, invest in hiring someone who does. In certain cases, it's always best to start with a trained expert. For instance, I would never want to see an ad hoc diversity, equity, and inclusion training by team members who aren't experts and/or certified in that topic. Be thoughtful in knowing what areas you can handle and which require professionals to facilitate.

How to Begin the Work

Step 1: Convene with purpose. When you conduct these ongoing meetings, use the practices listed in chapter 7. Set the tone by modeling meeting behaviors and structures that you want replicated.

Step 2: Review your data. To have a clear values focus, start by using the results from your Values Alignment Survey (chapter 5) as a tool for understanding where the team can start to make an impact. Focus your culture keeper efforts on the greatest areas of opportunity while also celebrating and lifting up what's working well.

Step 3: Host listening sessions. Listening session are similar to a focus group in that they are a type of facilitated discussion with a group of people aimed at collecting information about their experience. Participants in a listening session are asked to talk about what they know and think and to answer specific questions about a topic.

Listening sessions will enable you to learn the qualitative side behind the quantitative survey results. Sure, you may have the lowest scores with one of your values, but what does that really mean? You are truly making assumptions unless you talk to your people and get the stories behind the numbers.

When one of my clients went through this process, we learned that they had the best opportunity to be in greater alignment with their value of innovation. Because the team is relatively small, we had six of our culture keepers divide and conquer the staff list. Each one of them had an intimate conversation with a handful of team members to ensure that all voices were heard. By hosting small listening sessions, it created the opportunity for people to speak their truth and not feel overwhelmed and then go silent in a large company discussion.

Step 4: Share your results. Have your values leadership team reconvene and discuss what you heard to identify the lowest-hanging fruit and the opportunities to plan in a longer strategic effort.

Continuing with the previous example, we learned that there were clear trends, like the need for better technology, and that there were unique ideas, like having ongoing meditation sessions as a company. Some of it validated our instincts, and others were new concepts that we hadn't even considered. What was even better, though, was the surprise that each one of these culture keepers experienced along the way. They thought it was going to be like pulling teeth to get people to open up. They thought people would give mediocre responses and not be engaged in the process. And they (thankfully) were completely wrong. They were ultimately impressed, energized, and rewarded by these experiences and felt like they were truly a part of making a positive impact on their values alignment efforts within their culture.

Step 5: Create a values alignment plan. Now that you've gathered your qualitative and quantitative data, it's time to make a plan of action. Remember, this is not only about focusing on what's wrong but also about lifting up what's right. In determining your next steps, ask yourselves:

- How are we doing when it comes to living our values?

- What needs to change/evolve/shift in order for us to truly be grounded in these beliefs?

- What needs to be celebrated and lifted up as a proven culture keeper practice?

- What can we take action on immediately for team members to feel heard and understood?

- How can we create a long-term plan for change?

- What can we handle internally, and what do we need external support with?

- How can we communicate this process with the organization at large?

- How can we involve everyone in these opportunities to be in greater alignment?

- Where can we give ourselves and others more permission to be human?

It's up to you to decide how simple or robust this plan is. Perhaps you want to break it up with quarterly initiatives or to focus only on piloting a proven practice within a new department. You get to choose what makes the most sense for your team's capacity and commitment to knowing, owning, and living your values.

Step 6: Communicate your plan and results regularly. It's always a good idea to share your plan of action. That way, more people can step up to help and know what's expected of them along the way. Whenever you share, it's an opportunity to gain feedback and buy-in. Present your plan of action not only at its onset but also at a cadence in which it's regularly being discussed with your team. Perhaps you want it to be a standing line item on your monthly staff meeting, or maybe you want to create a separate meeting that's fully dedicated to the topic of values and culture.

Step 7: Rinse and repeat. Make sure that you're checking in with your alignment at least once a year. Then go through the steps outlined earlier to continue the iteration process. As you know by now, your culture exists every day whether you do something about it or not. When you intentionally check in and make meaningful adjustments, you're ahead of 90 percent of the companies out there.

Every single day, every single action is ultimately a reflection or disconnection of your values. When we give team members the power and opportunity to voice their perspectives, we can respond by showing them that we listened by making changes accordingly. When led with permission to be human, intention, and values alignment, these culture keeper programs have the power to support, heal, and grow your organization's strength now.

Permission to be human. Although the culture keeper idea is a wonderful one to nurture, we must also recognize that these people are humans with their own struggles and issues. We all have bad moments, days, or even weeks. The key is not only to ask that your culture keepers do more but also to support them in maintaining or enhancing their well-being in the process. Everyone will continue to benefit from those genuine high vibes. When your culture keepers become silent, lose their drive, or resign, it is a big warning sign that they're not being valued. Authentic enthusiasm and energy become evident when culture keepers are encouraged and supported in breeding hope, potential, and possibility.

In order for all those good vibes to be unleashed, we must activate the key concepts of conscious, mindful leadership. Simply put, someone who practices conscious, mindful leadership embodies presence by cultivating focus, clarity, and compassion in the service of others. Don't those sound like the qualities of the folks you want leading your team? Wouldn't you prefer your people to be mindful instead of mindless? Conscious instead of unconscious?

The following practical tips and tools are here to serve you and all your team members in being culture keepers every day by giving themselves permission to be human first, consciously igniting new levels of self-awareness, mindfulness, and feedback.

Activate Mindful Leadership

In addition to creating a culture keepers program to support the ins and out of crafting a values-aligned culture, it's just as important that all the humans in your workplace are taking care of their own well-being and sense of personal alignment. We all deserve to know about and build these skills so that we can live life on purpose. It's not your job as the owner or leader in your company to personally evolve each of your team member's sense of well-being. But it sure does send a powerful message when you embrace conscious, mindful leadership practices like these. As my mentor don Miguel Ruiz says often in his apprenticeship teachings, "When we change our own world, we can change the world around us."

- **Activate conscious mindfulness.** Mindfulness is the intentional act of curiously investigating the present moment. There's no judgment or pain when you're being mindful. You're simply being more aware by observing what's happening instead of being swept away by it. When you're mindful, you're not thinking about what didn't get done yesterday or how much you need to complete for tomorrow; you're just focusing on this present moment and are deeply tuned in to all that it has to offer.

Mindfulness also applies when planning for the future. Whether it's strategic planning, budgets, or even goal setting, we can be mindful in those future planning experiences by engaging in the process with intention. No texting or emailing while talking to your colleagues about the vision. Be fully there, and choose to be curious and active in observing what's coming up along the way.

- **Practice values-based mindfulness™.** After many years of living and teaching mindfulness, I wondered why there weren't mindfulness practices specifically based on our values. Because there wasn't a formal category for this type of practice, I created my own. Enter values-based mindfulness, which I define as "honoring one's core truth by making conscious choices that ignite a personal sense of alignment." Basically, what this entire book is about!

Living your values doesn't typically happen by chance. It happens when choosing your values with integrity over and over again. If you truly want to embrace your values in your daily habits, routines, and experiences, you must be mindful of whether you're living in alignment with them.

Something as simple as a full body check (where your mind, gut, and heart say yes) combined with your values filter will give you the information you need to make choices that serve you. For example, you might be having a really off day and want to understand where you're out of alignment with yourself.

> You can pop on one of my guided meditations on Insight Timer, or you can use your inner teacher to guide you.

Close your eyes; perhaps even put your hands on your heart. Take long, deep breaths to slow down, and simply ask yourself,

"Which one of my values can serve me now? How can I activate it with ease and grace in this moment?"

Happiness doesn't exist in the absence of our values. It's important to know how to tune in to understand how you can bring your values front and center into choosing your next steps. When we are honest with ourselves about what's out of alignment with our mind, body, and spirit, as well as with our sense of well-being, we have a real chance of getting back in alignment.

> In 2021, I launched my inaugural online values-based mindfulness cohort program, The Journey to Alignment.

It's a six-week quest of self-discovery to remember who you are at your core and to return to that place of personal alignment within. Through a combination of training modules and live group coaching, we explored what true core values alignment was when it came to managing emotional and physical energy as well as igniting healthy boundaries, habits, and routines that honor our heart's wisdom. It is a holistic approach to seeing life through the lens of our unique values and making choices that invite our values in and keep our frustrations out.

Watching these humans wake up to themselves has been one of the greatest honors of my life. I knew that these practices would serve them, but I didn't realize how quickly they'd be able to take big steps forward in setting boundaries with themselves, loved ones, and colleagues. I was blown away by their vulnerability in learning new techniques to connect to their heart, soul, and inner wisdom. And I was fueled with possibility when I heard story after story of how they felt new levels of peace, authenticity, and inner harmony as a result of intentionally choosing their values every day. One person finally set boundaries with their mother, another with their fiancé, and a third with their workplace. They all shared stories of using the tools to return to themselves in times when they felt completely out of control and harnessing them to feel a sense of grounding, power, and peace. Values-based mindfulness works, and you have the ability to access it anytime, because just like your breath, your values are always with you.

- **Stop suffering.** Eckhart Tolle says that there are two types of suffering: pain and fear. Pain is suffering from things that happened in the past. Fear is suffering from things that may or may not happen in the future.[52]

At work, pain can show up from a presentation that didn't go as well as you had hoped and during which one of your partners didn't have your back when you needed their support. Or a colleague who made you the brunt of a joke in a client meeting, making you feel like you had to smile your way through the embarrassment. Fear can show up as being hit with a major attack of imposter syndrome while preparing for a big presentation. Or not knowing whether you're going to lose your biggest client.

These are debilitating feelings that we're often hiding, and therefore we double down on suffering in silence. Through the following highlights, you'll learn powerful tools and tangible techniques to help you come back to the present moment and end your suffering.

- **Practice breath work.** When you find yourself in a situation where you've allowed your mind to take the wheel

---

52 Eckhart Tolle, *A New Earth: Awakening to Your Life's Purpose* (New York: Penguin Life, 2005), 32.

to pain and fear, go to your breath. You can only breathe right now—not in the past or in the future. When you can ground yourself in your breath, you are also grounding yourself in the present moment. And when you're mindfully in the present moment, suffering melts away. That can be as simple as paying attention to your breath.

Start by focusing on the intricacies of your breath (like the feeling of it going in and out of your nostrils, whether it is shallow or deep, the pace of it); this forces your mind to shut down the racket and be here now. You might even try imagining that there's a light following your breath in through the nostrils and down to the belly. Closing your eyes and watching your breath go in and out can be incredibly peaceful, as can repeating the mantras "I breathe in peace" on your inhale and "I breathe out stress" on the exhale. Just a few rounds of that repetition can make a massive shift in your inner grounding.

Finally, I recommend box breathing, which is also known as Navy SEAL breathing or tactical breathing because it's the technique that they use when in high-stakes situations. It's exactly as it sounds in that you create a box with your breath: inhaling for four counts, holding your breath for four counts, exhaling for four counts, holding for four counts. Simply repeat that pattern for one to two minutes, and see how much clearer your mind becomes and how your body eases.

> You can find guided practices in these techniques on Insight Timer.

- **Embrace meditation.** This practice is (thankfully) becoming more widespread, and study after study has proven its effect on people's well-being, focus, productivity, and relationships, to name a few areas.

  - A Detroit study looked at how meditation improved productivity in the workplace. It was found that absenteeism fell by 85 percent, productivity rose by 120 percent, and injuries dropped by 70 percent.[53]

  - Researchers at Boston University found that meditation programs had the ability to reduce anxiety and depression, making workers more optimistic and increasing their satisfaction with their careers.[54]

  - In a Harvard study, participants went through an eight-week mindfulness training program to determine the effects it had on focus. It was shown that meditation helped the subjects make faster and more attention-based adjustments, an ability that is very valuable in the workplace.[55]

  - Health-care company Aetna conducted a study with Duke to determine the return on investment of its

---

53 Jane E. Stevens, "Relaxing the Rules: More Companies Embrace Meditation: Businesses Say the At-Work Sessions Make for Happier Employees, Increased Productivity—Even Higher Profits," *Los Angeles Times,* June 5, 1995, https://www.latimes.com/archives/la-xpm-1995-06-05-ss-9814-story.html.

54 Thunderbird School of Global Management, "Benefits of Meditation in the Workplace," Arizona State University, November 29, 2017, https://thunderbird.asu.edu/knowledge-network/benefits-meditation-workplace.

55 Sue McGreevey, "'Turn Down the Volume': Meditation May Help the Brain Reduce Distractions," *Harvard Gazette,* April 22, 2011, https://news.harvard.edu/gazette/story/2011/04/turn-down-the-volume/.

mindfulness programming. Aetna figures that the productivity gains alone amounted to $3,000 per employee, an eleven-to-one return on its investment.[56]

- Organizations that introduce mindfulness programs see up to a 200 percent return on investment.[57]

Creating a daily meditation practice, if only for five minutes a day, will have a transformative influence on your life. I've had so many people tell me that they tried to meditate but that they didn't do it right because they had thoughts come up.

Michael Bernard Beckwith taught me that meditation is like a washing machine. You know how in the beginning of the wash cycle, the machine has to rumble your clothes in a way that releases the dirt from them? Well, the beginning process of meditation is the agitation cycle. All your thoughts (that "dirt") need to come up in order for them to ultimately be rinsed and released. Then after that agitation is complete, it's time for the rinse and clean stages. The key is to make it through the agitation to get there. This is precisely how meditation works.

The best teachers in meditation say if you have lots of thoughts, you're doing some of the greatest work, because you're allowing the space for them to be released.

There are loads of free apps, online trainings, and videos that are such great ways to start your practice. I highly recommend Insight Timer's Seven-Day Learn to Meditate free course to walk you through the basics of adopting your own practice.

---

56 David Gelles qtd. in B the Change, "Does It Pay Off? The True R.O.I. of Mindfulness in Business," May 17, 2016, https://bthechange.com/does-it-pay-off-the-true-r-o-i-of-mindfulness-in-business-3c9185dd8d11.

57 Search Inside Yourself Leadership Institute, "The ROI on Mindfulness in the Workplace," accessed January 15, 2021, https://siyli.org/resources/roi-mindfulness?gclid=EAIaIQobChMIx-W_g_HT5AIVIiCtBh2tqwJ3EAAYASAAEgJVZfD_BwE.

- **Use the "Just this" mantra.** Mantras are words or short phrases that can be used repeatedly to help you focus on your intention. The mantra "Just this" is a wonderful tool to help you close down the multitasking and focus in on just what you have in front of you. Even while writing this book, I'd find myself going off on tangents in my mind. I'd bring myself back to the work at hand by repeating to myself in my mind, "Just this." What might be possible in your life if you focused on just this?

- **Set intentions.** You've already heard me talk about intentions throughout the book. When it comes our own intentions (versus the intentions of a whole team), the opportunity becomes so much more personal. Consider setting intentions for your day, your meetings, your interactions, and your choices.

Before the start of an important meeting and especially on days with loads of meetings where I desire to stay grounded in the face of anxiety and chaos, I ring my energy chime. With one ding of the bell, I close my eyes and take deep breaths while reminding myself of why this meeting matters and what I intend to feel as a result of it. For example, I may say to myself in my mind, "This meeting matters because it's a chance for me to get on the same page with my team members after being away on vacation. I will feel reconnected and rejuvenated as a result." An energy chime is a simple tool that you can find easily online. Personally, I ring one that vibrates at a frequency that activates the heart chakra so that I can feel that heart connection in the process of choosing consciousness.

There's also a wonderful tool called the Five-Minute Journal (available in both app and hard copy form) that has a daily system for putting your top three intentions for the day. The developers frame it as "What will I do to make today great?" *These are intentions, my friends!* The more you can be precise and clear about what you want to experience, the more likely you will experience it.

- **Conduct a body scan.** Our bodies are the keepers of our souls, and they are constantly giving us powerful messages about what is OK and what is not. When we can make a deliberate effort to listen to our bodies and respond from a place of self-care, we can begin to be one with our mind, body, and spirit. There's a powerful Cherokee proverb that says, "If you listen to your body when it whispers, you won't have to hear it scream."

I can't tell you how many years I numbed out the whispers, ignored the signs, and popped a pill to get through. Today, when I notice my neck feeling stiff or have a headache coming on, I stop and check in with myself to see what I can do to tell my body that I heard it, that it matters, and that I will take care of it.

A body scan is an excellent tool for doing just that. It's the simple practice of closing your eyes (if you want) and slowly scanning your body from your head to your toes to see how it's doing. You can notice where you're tight, where you're feeling well, and then be intentional about giving yourself loving attention wherever your body could use it. A stretch, a walk, perhaps even a nap are great ways to start to build a kinder relationship with your body's whispers.

I have coached people with histories of migraines, massive shingles outbreaks, and even heart attacks who had been muscling their way through stress instead of slowing down and listening to what they needed to do to be healthy. One of my clients had her appendix burst and become infected in her body because she chose to ignore the pain and push on to meet her deadlines. Then after having emergency life-saving surgery, she came back to consciousness with her laptop, ready to get back to work from the hospital bed. You are not meant to just pay the bills and die. Don't let your work take over your ability to truly live a healthy and fulfilling life.

- **Take a technology detox.** We must disconnect from technology to reconnect to our humanity. Truly. We're not built to be staring at computer screens for extended periods of time. We're not built to be on Zoom all day long or scrolling on social media for hours on end, comparing ourselves to others. We must draw a hard line in the sand to determine what we need as individuals to be well and not consumed by technology. Perhaps you want to find a quitting time each day, where tech is off at 5:30 p.m., no exceptions! And especially not work emails when they are truly not an emergency. Or maybe you don't start to look at your phone until after you've been awake and taken care of your own needs for an hour.

Maybe you'd want to take it a step further and take retreats or vacations where you commit to divorcing from your tech while you're away. I often choose to go on retreats into the beautiful mountains of Idaho where I'm off the grid so that I can't cheat and check in when my ego starts to nag me to see what else is going on in the world.

- **Spend time in nature.** As humans, we are an expression of nature. Being one with nature is innate to us, yet many of us have become completely disconnected from that truth—especially when we live in places like bustling cities that don't have a lot of accessible nature nearby. Many people think that they're too busy to prioritize time in nature, or maybe they don't think they like it. If you happen to fall into those categories, know that nothing is wrong with you. Meet yourself where you are, and take baby steps to see what you might like and benefit from. Perhaps you'd consider an outdoor walking meeting instead of the usual office space? Or maybe you can take your lunch to a park and eat there by yourself or with others—it's always your choice how you use your breaks.

I have a really fun if-then policy. *If* a meeting gets canceled, *then* I go spend time in nature. Because I live in the city, that is usually a walk to my nearby park and back. While I'm there, I make a point to admire the trees and critters running around, take in the fresh air, and sometimes even take my shoes off and plant my feet in the earth for some grounding. So if an hourlong meeting gets canceled, I take a fifteen-minute walk in nature and still have forty-five more minutes to get back to work with greater clarity and focus after connecting with the wisdom of Mother Nature.

A simple thing like watching a bird take off and land on the very tip of a twig, the wind rustle the branches of the trees, bending them back but not breaking them, or even a bug carrying a huge chip on its back to feed its colony can be inspiriting and ignite new ideas, thinking, and possibilities for how to go about solving your own problems. There is a scientific process around this idea called biomimicry—which is a practice that learns from and mimics the strategies found in nature to solve human design challenges and find hope along the way.

- **Check your mindset.** There are two types of mindsets: abundance and scarcity. An abundance mindset is one that is rooted in love, believes in possibility, and is willing to see everything as a chance to grow, learn, and thrive. A scarcity mindset is one that is rooted in fear, believes there's not enough to go around, and is willing to give up when the going gets tough because there's too much to risk.

In the workplace, this can often be seen with competition. Let's say that you roll out a brand-new badass product that your team has spent an entire year developing. Then a few days later, you learn that a company, very similar to yours, just released its version of the same product.

What are you telling yourself about the current situation? Are you saying that it is impossible to be successful now? Or are you saying that it is a great opportunity for the market? If you're telling yourself it's impossible, then you'll get an impossible experience. But if you're telling yourself it's a great opportunity, then you'll be willing to roll up your sleeves and do the work that's required for that incredible opportunity that lives on the other side of it. The same goes for internal issues. If you have a top-performing team member who isn't seeing eye-to-eye with their supervisor, do you automatically huff and puff about how annoying people's issues are? Or do you see it as a chance to get to understand their perspectives and viewpoint more accurately?

- **Reframing.** Reframing is a technique used to help create a different way of looking at a situation, person, or relationship by changing its meaning. It is a transformative tool in every aspect of life.

One of the most powerful reframes I ever experienced was outside the workplace, with my grandma. She and my grandfather, Poppi, were in an assisted living facility in which people would move to different parts of the building depending on the level of care needed. There was an on-site medical area in which residents who were being treated stayed. It was also a place where many of the patients passed away. Poppi had passed away just a few weeks before my grandma had to be moved into that section of the facility. When I went to visit her, she was really overwhelmed and frightened because they had put her in the exact same section, room, and bed where her husband had just died. She was not OK. And then my aunt said to her, "Maybe this is Dad's way of keeping you close to him. Maybe this is how he's able to be in bed with you now as you heal." In an instant, her entire demeanor changed. She believed in that possibility and felt a new level of closeness to him, rather than fear. And quite frankly, it was what I needed to hear and believe in order to not file a complaint with management there. The ripple effects of a grounded reframe are significant.

At work, we might reframe failure as an opportunity for growth. A bad hire that was draining everyone of their sanity was what was needed to home in on the qualities that mattered most for that position. A lost client that you thought would be with you forever is an opportunity to learn where things need to improve for future clients. An embarrassing flub addressing your team can be exactly what you needed to show others that you're human, too, and can own your mistakes with grace. There is always a chance to reframe what you're experiencing in order to find the peace in the possibility on the other side of it.

This mindset work is about the vision, where we're headed—not being naive, with our heads in the sand, blinders on, embracing toxic positivity, but rather having a healthy frame to work toward the future from the lens of possibility.

- **Limiting Beliefs.** We are all served when we take the time to reflect on and identify our limiting beliefs. Any thought or idea that is holding you back from your potential is a limiting belief. In work, they often sound like this: "We're never going to be able to increase our profit this year." "Our staff is so needy." "This project will take forever." "There's not enough time for us to meet our goals." "Our culture will always be an issue."

Once you know your limiting beliefs, you can reframe your mindset and help others with theirs. If you happen to be in a conversation where people start to go down a path of negativity and lack, whether it's at work or anywhere else in your life, here are a few phrases you can try:

- "OK, so what's the possibility that lies within that opportunity?"

- "I'm curious about that, and I would love to continue that conversation at another time so that we can stay on track right now."

- "It feels like we're getting stuck in the weeds; let's reset together."

- "Now that I know why you think it won't work, give me three reasons why it might work."

- "I hear you and can relate. Let's recognize that as a challenge and build from it so that we don't get trapped there."

Another great way to work with your limiting beliefs is by finding evidence that it's possible to prove to yourself that what you've been telling yourself is not true. Say you have a limiting belief that it's not possible to be a CEO of a thriving business and also take vacation. That may feel very real to you right now in this moment when you look at everything that's stacked against you for truly getting time away. If you want to transform that limiting belief, you could actively seek out successful business leaders who share your values and who have mastered the art of vacationing. Get curious, ask questions, and be open to learning what they did to create that reality in their lives. Do whatever you can to acquire evidence that vacation is possible as a successful leader. Take action with what resonates with you.

This is the same concept as the when the four-minute mile record was broken. Before it happened, everyone thought it was impossible to run that fast. After it happened, it was only a matter of time before it was regularly broken because athletes knew that it was humanly possible.

- **Move from your head to your heart.** The majority of culture work is heart work, not head work. Most of us live in our heads and get stuck there all day long.

We can't find solutions in the same headspace in which they were created. When you have created a culture problem using your thinking mind, you may need to shift to your feeling heart in order to find a solution.

We all get stuck in our heads. We're taught to work harder, do more research, or think more deeply on it. What may be needed is for us to work at a slower pace, check in with ourselves and others more often, and feel more deeply.

There's a groundbreaking organization called HeartMath that has done extensive research on heart intelligence. I highly recommend that you check them out—especially if you're jazzed by data and science to prove that it's important for us to listen to our hearts. They provide several skill-building techniques to help people move from their heads to their hearts quickly. One of them is through something called a Quick Coherence Technique, which goes as follows:

- Step 1: Heart-focused breathing. Focus your attention in the area of the heart. Imagine that your breath is flowing in and out of your heart or chest area. Breathe a little slower and deeper than usual.

- Step 2: Activate a positive feeling. Make a sincere attempt to experience a regenerative feeling, such as appreciation or care, for something or someone in your life.[58]

This can take a minute or less and can have a massive transformative effect on your well-being. You may choose to do it publicly with your eyes closed and ask others to join you. Or do it anywhere you want without anyone being aware of what you're doing. While I was giving a keynote address, an audience member slung a question my way that completely undermined and demeaned what I had presented during the previous forty-five minutes. In the past, that would have been a jarring experience that made me put on a mask to be someone I wasn't in order to stay professional, not wanting to shut them down completely in their tracks. Instead, I was able to feel their energy coming my way, connect deeply with my heart at the very same time, and then envision that my heart was connecting and beating with theirs. That we were both humans who mattered and that what they were saying wasn't personal. In the end, they stayed after the talk to meet

---

58 HeartMath, "Quick Coherence® Technique," accessed August 22, 2020, https://www.heartmath.com/quick-coherence-technique/.

me, take a picture together, and thank me for hearing them and supporting their needs.

Slowing down to reconnect with your heart is an incredibly powerful way to honor the wisdom that it carries—the wisdom that we all carry as a human race. Reconnecting with your heart and the hearts of your team members can change the entire way you run your business for the better.

When I am working with teams of highly analytical and data-driven people, there can be a hesitation with these types of exercises. They don't want me to facilitate something that might make people feel uncomfortable, which I get. But what's unfortunate is that they're also unwilling to see what might be possible for their people when they try. I've done heart-centering practices with firefighters, cybersecurity teams, engineers, computer programmers, and doctors across practically all generations. I'm always left feeling so hopeful when they openly share how close minded they were at first and how much better they felt when they tried the mindfulness exercises.

The point here is to nurture the values-based practices you've worked hard to build up, whether through a culture keepers program or mindful leadership practices. Every ounce of energy spent on slowing down, to see where you're mindful or practicing mindfulness, will ultimately get you further ahead in activating a whole team of people who can do the same. For value promises to seep into the very sinew of your organization, you must engage the body, and the heart in particular, as well as the mind through your values work.

Your culture keepers programs and team members will be there to ignite that embodiment with purpose. You'll link arms and step forward together into the horizon of potential, knowing that you'll keep one another lovingly accountable to behaving in alignment with your shared company core values. You're not alone, and you're better together.

If you're someone who's hesitant about this kind of work, try it out in your own life and lean on your fellow culture keepers to celebrate wins, talk through sticking points, and get curious with your questions. Take one practice at a time, give it a genuine shot, then decide if it's something that will make its way into your personal tool kit. It's easy for me to advocate for these things because of the tremendous effect they've had on my own life and the lives of those I've worked with. At the same time, one size does not fit all. The point is that you keep adding to your tool kit, swapping tools out and sharing them with others who could benefit from their power.

Values Alignment Review

1. When led with permission to be human, intention, and values alignment, culture builder programs have the power to support, heal, and grow your organization's strength now.

2. Someone who practices conscious, mindful leadership embodies presence by cultivating focus, clarity, and compassion in the service of others.

3. Values-based mindfulness is honoring one's core truth by making conscious choices that ignite a personal sense of alignment.

4. Reframing is a technique used to help create a different way of looking at a situation, person, or relationship by changing its meaning.

5. The majority of culture work is heart work, not head work. When you have created a culture problem using your thinking mind, you may need to shift to your feeling heart in order to find a solution.

This chapter highlighted our:
- Guided meditations on Insight Timer
- The Journey to Alignment six-week values alignment cohort program

If any of these opportunities sparked your interest, learn more at www.permissiontobehuman.co, or check out the SparkVision Resources section of this book.

CHAPTER 10

Conclusion

Keep your thoughts positive because your thoughts become your words.
Keep your words positive because your words become your behavior.
Keep your behavior positive because your behavior becomes your habits.
Keep your habits positive because your habits become your values.
—Mahatma Gandhi

Giving yourself permission to be human is hard. Giving an entire organization, including yourself, permission to be human can be even harder. That's because as human beings, we are incredibly complex. We have preferences and pet peeves, tendencies, and habits. We have egos and fear, personalities, and love. We have stories of the past that shape narratives of the present and future. We have things that bring us joy and things that make us recoil. These are all combined with generational trauma and ancestral power. And although we are more similar than different, values were all taught to and instilled in us in distinct ways. Whether we're at work, at home, on vacation, or running errands, whether we honor the truth of our human complexities or pretend that they're not real, all this (and a heck of a lot more) lives inside of us.

We've been programmed by the people responsible for domesticating us as children—our parents, teachers, friends, media. For many, many generations, we've created these societal rules that said things like, "Work must be at least forty hours a week to be valuable," "Hustle, hustle, hustle," "Your personal stuff doesn't belong at work," or "Emotions don't belong in the boardroom." We've wrapped up so much of our identities in the titles of our jobs, the success of our business, and the amount of money we make. But so many of us find that in the end, our work was something we simply did as a way to make it through life or check approval boxes from others, to work for the weekend and hang on to the dream of what our lives would be like in retirement. E. E. Cummings said it best: "It takes courage to grow up and become who you really are."

It takes courage and loyalty to yourself to step up to do the deep work to truly understand your gifts and the values that surround them in order to intentionally create a workplace experience that makes you feel alive and aligned each day. You're fortunate to realize that you can make that choice, knowing that if you can do better for yourself, you can be the example for everyone else to do the same in whatever that means, through their own lens. We're not all built to do the same thing. That's what makes all those preferences and stories and habits and histories so very important.

This courageous path of a culture keeper is one that will have many hurdles. There will be days when everything will feel like the puzzle pieces of your culture are finally locked into place and then someone comes and flips the table on you, and you must pick up all the pieces. The beauty reveals itself when you feel like you've lost it but then the curious, trained, and caring humans around you show up and get down on the floor next to you. They help you sort out the mess and reassemble your vision into reality, one piece at a time. That is when you've developed a culture where people have permission to be human and are held accountable to aligning with your shared core values.

I witnessed this so powerfully a few years ago with my dear friend Jennifer Rotner's company, Elite Creative. Completely out of the blue, they lost over 50 percent of their revenue from their primary client. Only one month earlier, this very client had asked them to ramp up their staffing to take on more work. Believing this would be the case, they made their biggest focus as a company to scale their operations in preparation for meeting their future demand. Basically, this client became all-consuming of their time, people, and resources, as is the case with behemoth clients like this, but the rest of the company became pretty stagnant. So when the client pulled the rug out from underneath them, it felt like they had nothing left.

Jennifer was completely sideswiped by the news; this client had essentially dismantled and shut down the whole arm of her services that was keeping her business thriving. The team felt the immense hit of pressure, stress, and anxiety, and they rallied the troops, came up with innovative new solutions and lines of business, and were all in to see it through. They had to lay off a significant amount of their ramp-up team, but everyone understood the decision because of how humanely they handled the process—with transparency and grace.

Within only a few months of having flipped the whole business on its head, they developed an entirely new branch, replaced their lost revenue, and even hired back a significant portion of their team. It was through their core values of adaptability, trust, and magic that they stood strong in the face of adversity and pulled through. They bounced back almost fully in the first year, doubled in company size and revenue in the second year, and doubled again in size and revenue in the third year. Notably, during the first two years, they had 100 percent retention of their full-time employees, including all the senior staff. Expanding at lightning speed, with the growing pains that come with that, the team stayed the course. The year it all went down, Jennifer was even named one of the most admired CEOs in the state of Maryland. The reason why this all worked out was because they were a well-oiled culture-keeping machine long before this crisis emerged.

When they host "culture calls" with new full-time team members, they always include the story of what happened then and how they all banded together. Jennifer said, "It's become part of our mythology and something we proudly carry with us. I feel like as a team, we were forged by fire, and there's nothing we can't accomplish together."

Their leadership invests tremendously in annual off-site, overnight retreats where everyone is appreciated to the max while also problem-solving and team building. Although each of these experiences has a work/strategy element, the main focus is creating once-in-a-lifetime experiences. Jennifer's goal is to blow their minds and leave them with wonderful memories and bonding experiences. On the senior leadership retreats specifically, she works with intention to play to each person's interests and find ways to make them feel special and appreciated.

They have strong core values and live them wholeheartedly—not only on fancy retreats but also when the going gets tough. There was never a moment when I was concerned for her team because I had witnessed over many years how deeply invested they were with one another as humans.

I can't tell you how many days I throw my hands up in the air and ask myself why the heck I chose such a complicated and heavy profession. And then I remind myself that those heavy days are worth it because on the other side of them are even more days that bring hope, promise, possibility, and growth.

This is not to say that every experience has a happy ending. It's quite the contrary. You *must* listen to the struggle, honor it, and meet yourself in that place to make conscious, values-based, mindful choices that will lead you and your team to true values alignment.

We can't fix people, and we can't fix culture. That's simply and completely the wrong mindset. We take a seat next to the people creating culture and listen. Then we do what's needed to heal, evolve, adapt, and shift the culture to serve the vision, mission, and values of our organization. When you're a leading culture keeper, it's your responsibility to look in the mirror, do the work, and help yourself first. Then light your torch of wisdom and illuminate a path of possibilities for others to help themselves on. Point out the obstacles, and do your best to not fix or judge. Keep igniting more torches so that they can carry their own light forward into a path of personal well-being and values alignment. When you give yourself and others permission to be human, your life and the lives you've touched will have more meaning.

Mantras and Affirmations

As you move through your journey in embodying the qualities of a conscious, values-aligned, mindful culture keeper, I want to provide you with a list of powerful reminders in the form of mantras and affirmations.

> You might appreciate our Values-Alignment Card Deck that accompanies these and provides some deeper reflection, or you might just want to pull your favorites and put them on a sticky note by your computer screen.

If you have only a short time for this exercise, remember the Culture Keeper Credo:

I choose to be a culture keeper and not a killer.

I am a conscious, grounded, mindful leader.

I own the energy I create in the world.

My behaviors reflect our values and ignite purpose in my life.

When out of alignment, I hold myself and others lovingly accountable.

And in doing so, I give myself and my team permission to be human.

If you have a longer period to focus on these mantras, think about the broader landscape of values-aligned work.

Chapter 1: The Evolution of Workplace Culture

+ I am aware of my energy and how it impacts others.

+ I am a walking, talking, living, breathing set of values.

+ My energy shows me when my values are present.

+ I nurture and sustain the culture around me.

- I create a sense of purpose, connection, and belonging with my team.

Chapter 2: Being a Human at Work

- I nurture trust and empowerment.

- I ignite psychological safety, vulnerability, and a sense of purpose with others.

- I find wisdom in my wounds.

- I gain confidence, skills, and knowledge by trying and learning.

- Culture change starts with me.

- I am willing to do the deep work.

Chapter 3: How Values and Behaviors Create Culture

- My core values are my internal compass and represent what I stand for.

- I honor my values and the role they play in my life.

- Values reflect who we are, what we do, and how we define success and failure.

- Every day is filled with purpose, pride, and productivity when our values are activated.

- My behaviors are my values in action.

- I choose to change my behaviors to better align with my values.

Chapter 4: Knowing Your Personal Values

- I know my values and what motivates me.

- I am mindful of what does and does not activate my values.

- I honor my past to align my future.

- I expand my awareness to embrace my values.

- When I know who I am, I can truly know who others are.

Chapter 5: Knowing Your Company Values

- Together, we create our shared core values.

- I listen to others to understand their intrinsic motivators.

- Our values are ours to define.

- We celebrate our values.

- Our values serve as our compass and guardrails for success.

Chapter 6: Value Promises

- We own our values.

- We keep our promises.

- Expectations – Agreement = Disappointment

- Expectations + Agreement = Satisfaction

- Honoring my humanity helps others grow on their journey.

Chapter 7: How to Integrate Values into Cultural Norms

- We know, own, and live our values through our actions.

- We make values-aligned, grounded decisions with clarity.

- I praise more than I criticize.

- Curiosity is the cure for all frustration.

- I share my intent before sharing content.

- We engage people through our values.

- We appreciate, recognize, and celebrate our team.

Chapter 8: How to Integrate Values into Operations

- We invest in what we value.

- We teach our values so that we can live our values.

- Our operations reflect our values.

- I take values violations seriously.

Chapter 9: Building Conscious Culture Keepers through Mindfulness

- I cultivate focus, clarity, and compassion in the service of others.

- I curiously investigate the present moment.

- I choose my values in the face of adversity.

- My breath anchors me in this moment.

- My happiness exists in the presence of my values.

- Just this.

- I disconnect from technology to reconnect with my humanity.

- I live in abundance.

- I reframe my experience to see the possibilities.

- I slow down to get ahead.

Whether every single one of these resonated with you or only a few seemed like keepers, make a choice as to how these mantras and affirmations might benefit you as friendly reminders—both proactively and reactively. I hope these will serve you in your journey in knowing, owning, and living your values and be a reflection of how exquisite it is to choose the never-ending journey of being a conscious leader.

Claiming Our Superpowers

As a kid, I wanted to be a superhero like my mom. But I'm not her, and I needed to follow my own path. I didn't think it was possible after years of being knocked down by toxic cultures, feeling doomed to just accept the norm. I didn't know how much my energy had powered and influenced the environments around me. There wasn't anyone telling me otherwise, but they were always ready to finish a bottle of wine and complain about work woes together.

And you know what? After years of choosing to be a victim, I finally woke up and realized that I needed to give myself permission to be human and start making choices and setting boundaries that served my well-being and aligned with my values. Then, like fireflies in the night, I started to see so many people around me light up and begin taking steps on their own paths to authenticity.

When I started my business, I knew that it would be built on the foundation of my values and would intentionally foster a culture that gave everyone I engaged with permission to be human. Like my former colleague and friend told me (in chapter 2) when I knew I had to leave my job to start my own company, I wasn't willing to bend over anymore and pretend like it didn't hurt. It was finally my chance to build the floor in a way that wouldn't hurt my back or cause me to lose anything. Within months of making the transition to entrepreneurship, national organizations were seeking out my services without advertising. It wasn't because of some fancy methodology, degree, or research. It was because the people in my world felt that permission to be human when we were together—and they wanted more. When you connect with someone on a heart level, it's hard to forget it. Conscious leaders want to bring those experiences to their own people.

And now, every day, I can proudly claim that I get to be a conscious, values-driven, mindful, intrinsically aligned superhero by giving people permission to be human. It starts from within. Every time I make space to heal my own wounds, I open space for those around me to do the same. Every time I admit my failures and apologize, I invite others to join me. Every time I can empathize and relate to someone who's sharing vulnerably, I show them it's safe to speak their truth. This all ignites more and more possibility. Helping team members feel heard so that they can finally sleep at night to empowering someone to use their voice to tell their supervisor what's not working to encouraging a manager to celebrate someone who is putting in the work to grow—I am a culture-keeping superwoman!

This is an attainable superpower for all of us—not a special gift some of us were born with and others were not.

What is special is making the choice to align my energy and actions with my values. Choosing to attract people together instead of push them apart. Choosing to say the things that are hard because they're what's right. *And guess what?* You have that exact same power and choice to make every day.

You can go from being a culture killer to a culture keeper, a disconnected executive to a connected one, a value novice to a values expert by making a different choice. A belief exists only as long as you say yes to it. As soon as you say no, a new possibility is born. It can be that simple. You're meant to go on a journey to know, own, and live your values so that your life, team, and company can thrive.

Now you get to choose. Will you become a conscious, values-driven, behavior-aligned, culture keeping superhero in your organization?

Values Alignment Review

This chapter highlighted our Values Alignment Card Deck.

If it sparked your interest, learn more at www.permission-tobehuman.co, or check out the SparkVision Resources section of this book.

Acknowledgments

I knew writing a book would be an exciting new muscle to strengthen, but I had no clue that it would be the most vulnerable experience of my life. It's one thing to share something with a small group or in a piece of online writing that could later be edited, and it's something entirely different to spend over a year pouring your heart into hundreds of pages with the intention for it to translate into love and possibility for others. Thankfully, I was writing a book about giving permission to be human, so I was constantly reminded to take my own medicine when imposter syndrome, doubt, and unworthiness bubbled up throughout the process. In the end, it was the humans who walked this journey alongside me who ultimately served as my mirror to release my fears and surrender to love.

There are so many people to thank for their love and support through it all. I must begin with my husband and truest embodiment of a partner in life. James, you held space for me in my lows and insisted that we celebrate the highs. You unconditionally listened to me read every single word of this book out loud (over and over again) and provided such stellar feedback that no one else would have been able to give but you. You know my heart so well, and I'm forever grateful that you helped to ensure it was heard in my words here. I love you with all my being and can't wait to see where this journey takes us next.

I offer a deep bow of gratitude:
To the team at Modern Wisdom Press, who held each other's hands as we birthed our first books together. Catherine and Nate, your guidance, facilitation, and heart-centered approach to being a channel in writing was a gift that will keep on giving every time I sit down to express myself. I had no idea that I would need that communal support to remind me of my own humanity through our shared experience. Kari, Mike, and Billy, you have been with me (even from afar) every step of the way on this journey, and I'm a better person for it. I'm proud of us all for doing this author thing.

To the team at Elite Creative, who painstakingly worked with me as a brand-new author who had no idea what I was doing. Jenny Rotner, you're such a star in my life. So high up, constantly shining light down on my uncharted path, especially in the darkest skies. The encouragement, nurturing, and energy you poured into making sure that this book was edited at the highest caliber was some of the most soothing balm on my most vulnerable spots in this process. Thank you for being my loyal soul sister and fierce advocate in my life.

To my friend and cherished partner, Charles Johnson-Bey, for believing in me and supporting my vision since the start. The foreword you lovingly wrote for this book was a gift to my soul. How thankful I am that we get to experience this lifetime together by doing good work and having fun along the way. You are the epitome of excellence in all that you commit to.

To David Swirnow for trusting me with his team to ignite a values-driven culture and for providing the direct inspiration for the naming of this book. It's exactly the sentiment I intended, and you found the words to express that. It's amazing to think how far we've come and the depth of our partnership in work and life.

To Jennifer McDowell, Jordan Goodman, Christina Moniodis, Matt Bralove, and Kesha Simone-Jones for adding your invaluable perspectives and insights to this book—and for doing it with love and grace. Jennifer, you single-handedly saved chapter 5! What a gift to have humans in your corner who want to see you shine.

To Julie Reisler, Jon Berghoff, Enrique Rubio, and Darlene Slaughter for getting your hands on the book early and for quickly trusting its content to provide advance praise. Your backing is profound. And to Lisa Schroeder, who provided advance praise and incredibly rich content for this book after years of meaningful partnership together. My life is simply and completely better because you are a part of it.

To the Smith Publicity team for immediately making me realize that I can get so much further when we partner with experts. After connecting with Marissa, Janet, and Shannon, I just knew that our values were in sync and that together we're going to make a big splash. And to my soul sister, Kait LeDonne, for connecting me and teaching me how to harness my voice for good on LinkedIn. I feel like you set me up for this moment years ago, and I can do anything with you in my corner.

To Lou Goines for rolling up her sleeves and pulling her editing wisdom out of retirement to ensure my baby was taken care of. I'm so grateful that we are chosen family. You and Richard have been among the greatest silver linings in our lives during this upside-down time. Thank you for being my self-proclaimed number one fan and raving supporter in life.

To all the communities that give me permission to be human and to all of those that did not, thank you for showing me what that feels like. It all started with ELU and has now expanded into our Masterminds and BWON tribes. You're all a constant source of support and inspiration. And to my Values Heart Trust (formally known as my Life Lens Brain Trust), who have been with me since my values work was just a passion project that I offered in my spare time. You've given me constructive and affirming feedback with each evolution of this work, guiding me toward the greatest possibilities. Your hearts, minds, spirits, and values inspired me as these pages were filled.

To all the teachers, researchers, mentors, guides, and groundbreakers who paved the way for this moment in our history where people are starting to truly understand why our human experience matters at work. I hope my references to your work throughout this book recognize you for the impact you're making in this world.

Finally, I am forever grateful to every family member and confidant who has made and continues to make me such a wealthy soul by pouring your love into me. Thank you for igniting such profound abundance in my life.

About the Author

As the founder and chief visionary of SparkVision, MaryBeth Hyland knows that extraordinary success is rooted in the vision, values, and culture crafted by purpose-driven leaders and their tribe. With over a decade of experience built on knowledge from a BA in social work and an MS in nonprofit management, she is recognized for her ability to guide individuals and teams to know, own, and live their values.

And she does that with the understanding that we all have a deep desire to know and return to our most authentic selves—at work, at home, and within.

As a consultant, mindfulness instructor, and values expert, she engages audiences and teams all over the world with her humanistic style of facilitation, coaching, and empowerment.

Her recent awards include the *Daily Record*'s Circle of Excellence, Innovator of the Year, Top 100 Women, Leading Women, and Associated Black Charities' Civic Engagement Leader. She also has been recognized as a leading expert by the *Washington Post*, *Huffington Post*, *Forbes*, the *Wall Street Journal*, and more.

Her life mission is to create spaces where voices are heard, stories are released, and purpose is ignited.

Further Reading

Brown, Brené. *Dare to Lead: Brave Work. Tough Conversation. Whole Hearts.* New York: Random House, 2018.

Covey, Stephen. *The Speed of Trust: The One Thing That Changes Everything.* New York: Free Press, 2006.

Coyle, Daniel. *The Culture Code: The Secrets of Highly Successful Groups.* New York: Bantam, 2018.

Godin, Seth. *Tribes: We Need You to Lead Us.* New York: Penguin Group, 2008.

HeartMath. "Quick Coherence® Technique." Accessed August 22, 2020. https://www.heartmath.com/quick-coherence-technique/.

Lee, Sophie. "40-Hour Work Week: The History and Evolution." Culture Amp. Accessed September 9, 2020. https://explore.cultureamp.com/c/40-hour-work-week-th?x=MdEi_K.

Manyika, James, Susan Lund, Michael Chui, Jacques Bughin, Jonathan Woetzel, Parul Batra, Ryan Ko, and Saurabh

Sanghvi. "Jobs Lost, Jobs Gained: What the Future of Work Will Mean for Jobs, Skills, and Wages." McKinsey Global Institute. November 28, 2017. https://www.mckinsey.com/featured-insights/future-of-work/jobs-lost-jobs-gained-what-the-future-of-work-will-mean-for-jobs-skills-and-wages.

Porath, Christine. *Mastering Civility: A Manifesto for the Workplace.* New York: Grand Central, 2016.

Schwartz, Shalom H. "An Overview of the Schwartz Theory of Basic Values." *Online Readings in Psychology and Culture* 2, no. 1 (December 2012). https://doi.org/10.9707/2307-0919.1116.

Tolle, Eckhart. *A New Earth: Awakening to Your Life's Purpose.* New York: Penguin Life, 2005.

SparkVision Resources

The intention of this book is to ignite new possibilities within yourself and your team in terms of aligning your behaviors with your values. Some readers may be advanced facilitators already whereas others may be completely new to this conversation. As such, we've designed a variety of ways you can further develop your values-based mindfulness skills to ignite a thriving culture around you.

Go to permissiontobehuman.co for more information on the following:

- **Know and Live Your Values audio course.** This ten-day online course on the Insight Timer platform is accessible twenty-four seven and only takes fifteen minutes a day to identify your unique values, see where you're currently activating them, and make small tweaks where you're not. This awareness will provide a new lens through which you can experience your life with intention. It's the perfect on-demand guide to enhance the teachings in chapter 4.

- **Insight Timer.** This is a free global meditation and mindfulness app that you can access anytime. In addition to the course outlined above, I also provide free values-based mindfulness guided meditations and talks. You can check them all out on insighttimer.com/marybeth.hyland, or search my name within the app itself.

- **The Journey to Alignment.** This six-week cohort program is for individuals who are on a quest of self-discovery to remember who you are at your core and return to that place of personal alignment within.

- **The Community of Alignment.** Join a sacred community or chosen family to support you on the lifelong journey to know, own, and live your values.

- **Values Retreats.** We offer a variety of Values Retreats with an expert facilitator for both individuals from the community and workplace teams who are eager to know, own, and live their values. They range from half-day experiences to multiday engagements. Essentially, we take all the work from chapters 4–6 and guide you through it in real time together.

- **Permission to Be Human Online Course.** Designed to accompany this book, our online course dives deeper into the work outlined throughout each of the ten chapters. The online modules can be completed at your own pace coupled with biweekly live group coaching to support your specific questions, sticking points, and celebrations.

- **Values Alignment Card Deck.** We take all the mantras outlined in chapter 10 coupled with reflection questions to ponder and take action on. They are woven into a beautifully designed card deck to create more intention and fun with daily opportunities to align behaviors with your values.

- **Values Alignment Guide Apprenticeship.** To fully embody the work, it takes a loving accountability, willingness to do the hard work, and openness to the coaching needed to become a person who authentically lives in alignment with their values. That is precisely why I developed an apprenticeship program for people who feel called to activate their own gifts to further support others in their journey to alignment at work, home, and within. Becoming an apprentice is a commitment for both the teacher and the student. As such, this is a boutique experience for a small group of passionate culture keepers who see the benefit in being certified to share this work with others.

We offer even more support through workshops, one-on-one coaching, and keynote presentations. Check out www.sparkvisionnow.com to see it all!

And please, connect with me on LinkedIn (www.linkedin.com/in/marybethhyland/) and let me know what you thought of the book, or just follow me for consistent sharing on ways to truly embrace your values in work, life, and within.

Cheers to the possibilities!

9 781737 288817